# *BOTTOMLESS BAGGIE*

by Karl Rohnke

KENDALL/HUNT PUBLISHING COMPANY
2460 Kerper Boulevard P.O. Box 539 Dubuque, Iowa 52004-0539

**Cover:** Lineart illustration by Plynn Williams

Copyright © 1991 by Karl E. Rohnke

ISBN 0-8403-6813-5

Printed in the United States of America
10 9 8 7 6 5 4 3 2 1

# Bottomless Baggie

## Table of Contents

# *DISCLAIMER*

*It is important to remember that:*

- The opinions and ideas expressed in this book are the property and responsibility of the author alone and should not be attributed to any other individual or organization.

- Adventure curricula or activities should not be undertaken without the supervision of leaders who have successfully completed qualified professional instruction in the use of the skills necessary to implement adventure curricula or activities.

- Instruction and suggestions in this book for the construction and implementation of ropes course elements are subject to varying interpretations and the construction process is an inexact science.

- Before any attempt is made to use any ropes course elements whose construction has incorporated any of the materials contained in this book, a qualified professional should determine that safe techniques have been employed in their construction thereafter.  Inspections by a qualified professional no less frequently than annually should be made to protect users against accident or injury that can result from the deterioration of materials caused by the use, abuse or the elements.

- The reader assumes all risk and liability for any loss or damage which may result from the use of the materials contained in this book. Liability for any claim, whether based upon errors or omissions in this book or defects in any ropes course the construction of which has incorporated any of the materials contained in this book shall be limited in amount to the purchase price of this book.

# *Bottomless Baggie Intro*

There's no way I'm going to wait another ten years to write/edit **The Bottomless Bag** sequel.  I remember what it was like collecting, editing, and rewriting the first 38 issues; I'm not about to do that again.

Recently, however, I noticed that 2-1/2 years of *Bag of Tricks* have gone by since *Bottomless Bag* was first printed in 1988:  hard to believe.  Considering that 2-1/2 years equates to ten 12-page issues, and subtracting about 2 pages per issue (mailing info, topical issues, less than neat-o items, newsiness), that comes out to about 100 pages of text to edit and rewrite; or a 75% improvement over 400 pages.

About 912.5 days from now, I'll probably be numbed as to the hassles of this first, in what I hope will be a series of sequels — *Bottomless Baggies* 1, 2, 3, etc.  I agree that "moderation is for monks," but no more triple-century page tomes like THIS ONE for me.  Go for; less than long, semi-sweet, and to the blunted point — in 100 pages or less.

If none of the above makes any sense, be of good cheer, I become more lucid as the responsibility of expository content becomes chaptered and paginated.

## *Newsy stuff for faithful readers...*

Bonnie Hannable is still digitizing *BOT's* for me each quarter and has agreed (obviously) to format the material in this booklet.  Yeah Bonnie!

Drew (younger son) still helps each quarter with the mechanics of getting out the copy.  His greatest mailroom concern continues to be a morbid fear of getting a paper cut on his tongue from licking envelopes; so I bug him by swiftly sliding the gummy part of the sealing flap up and down on my tongue, and garbling, "Shum on Drew, le's rache."

For all those people who said I would eventually start using a word processor, you may heap my psyche with multiple, "I-told-you-so's."  I have finally given in, and do most of my writing and editing on a Mac — although right now (I mean RIGHT NOW), I'm scribing with a ballpoint pen and yellow pad, and the old Royal portable is close at hand.

There are multiple Macs and mouses at the Project Adventure office in Wenham, MA, and a plethora of cursory ex-pats extolling their virtues. These nouvous digitizers are insidious in their relentless (and I think subconscious) quest to subvert typers and scribers to become like them — kind of like the movie *Invasion of the Body Snatchers*. Toward the end of my fairly childish period of resistance to computers, I sometimes felt like running from room to room yelling, "Don't let them get you — they're everywhere." Well, they are and they did. But the machine is easy to use and does what it's supposed to, if I do what I'm supposed to. I take some compensation in that I still don't know how to *really* use the thing, and if you are a user, you know what I mean. But be of good cheer, keepers of the pen, I still digitally abuse the Royal on a regular basis.

People continue to be very generous with their ideas, sending them to me on a regular basis. I try to include as many received ideas as I can within the fairly compact format of *BOT's*, and also give credit when my filing system works. So thanks, I appreciate your generous sharing of ideas, and I'm sure other readers are benefiting from your experiential largesse.

I have no idea how much longer I will continue producing the quarterly periodical **Bag of Tricks**; I guess when the collecting, writing, and sharing is no longer satisfying. The number of subscribers as of December 1990 is just over 500, representing a recent jump from the 300 or so that had been consistent for years. I guess adventure programming is catching on. If you are one of the folks who just caught on, or you're a faithful *BOT's* subscriber, welcome to another atypical anthology of fun, frolic, fantasy, and frenetic folderol.

I would like to thank the following people for the following things.

Bonnie Hannable again, for all the things listed on the second turnable page of **The Bottomless Bag.** How come there's no number on that page? I should do something about that.

Plynn Williams for designing another entertaining book cover, and for various cartooning and illustrative reconstructions.

No one has read over the text material for this book except me, which is why I would like you to really read the disclaimer that precedes the text; no fair just perusing. I have tried my best to include only those activities that are fun, functional, and safe, but any activity is only as safe as the practitioner's presentation. If in doubt (about safety), don't do it. Sign up for a Project Adventure workshop, and get some hands-on experience about how all this stuff works, physically and conceptually.

## Chapter One
# *Adventure Games*

**Snatch It**

Linda Kelly, PA Trainer from Colorado, passed along this satisfyingly rude activity. See also "Cranial Snatch It," under **Stunts**, Chapter 4, pg. 68.

Grab a few "knee-highs" or whacked-off sections of pantyhose from your *Comet Ball* collection and put an unweighted tennis ball down into the toe of the sock. Put the other end (the open end) over your head, so that the sock fits like a skull cap. You are now ready to play...and establish a new fashion statement.

The object of play is to snatch the cap from another player and continue to do this until you are the last player remaining — cap intact. The "winner" can either be that last person or you can introduce a scoring system as follows. You get one point for each "scalp" you capture and three additional points if you are the last unscalped player. The most effective scalper is obviously that snatcher with the most points at game's end.

*Caveats* — I'm inclined to suggest only playing if you use the longer pantyhose (not knee-highs) on your head. This puts the snatchable end somewhere around the sternum and keeps fingers away from the face and eyes.

Try out this game with an older group of students before you introduce it to a younger, less controllable group.

**Knee Slap**

Last week, I was up at Dartmouth's Ravine Lodge in New Hampshire (near Mt. Moosilauke) doing my annual game and initiative thing. About 15 exchange students from the University of Moscow (right, the USSR Moscow) were there doing something else. Just before starting the games workshop, we decided to invite the Soviets to join us and, happily, they did for the morning session. And it **was** a happy time. Language barriers are

1

easily overcome by play. Anyway, during the session, one of the Soviet women showed me this knee-slapper activity that I think you will like as much as we did at the time.

Sit in a circle, close enough to one another so that you can easily put your hand on the knee of the person next to you. Do that now, making sure that your arms are crossed with the person to your right and left. As you look at your hands and the hands of the people next to you, it's a bit confusing to tell whose hand is whose, and there's the crux of the activity. If you need some patter to overcome any initial knee-grabbing resistance, say this, "Put your arms out in front of you, palms down. Move your arms out to right and left so that your hands are over the knees of the persons next to you. Lower your hands and gently grab those knees."

Because some people do not have much forward flexibility, you might find that sitting in the above L-shaped configuration might be painful to impossible for them. If you find that's the case, have everyone stand, and go for a knee in that half standing position. Not as relaxed a position, and it's kind of hard to see what's going on — but considering what you are doing, that's not all bad either. Now, go for it.

Begin a hand-slap-of-the-knee sequence by simply and gently slapping the knee of the person to your right. Then, continue the hand-knee slapping from person to person, *trying to do so without slapping out of sequence.* Try to go faster and faster. Try to start the sequence in both directions. Try not to laugh.

## All Catch

This simple game was passed along by Dave Villandry of Cambridge, MA, (quite a gamesman himself).

Have the group stand in a group so that they aren't touching each other, unless they want to, and if they do, you better have another game in mind 'cause this one involves no touching.

One ball (any size, made of soft stuff) is tossed up to a height of about 10 feet. If the ball is caught by someone, a second ball is introduced; i.e., two balls are thrown up simultaneously by two different people. If both balls are caught (not by the person who threw it), then a third ball is introduced. The object is to include as many balls as possible into the throwing pattern until someone drops one. If a ball is dropped, start over again. Balls must be thrown simultaneously on command.

As 2, 3, and 4 balls are put into play, unless some group strategy is developed, the random throws often all plop down in the same area with a predictable dropped ball result. It's the same concept that makes the game *Quail Shooter's Delight,* a.k.a. *Phones & Faxes,* function through failure.

**Shoe Bin**

Simplistic? Old? Yeah, I guess, but as the result of a recent try at this well-known primary party game, I'm more inclined to take a second look at some other "marginal" activities that I have mentally shelved or circle-filed. (See *Barnyard* in this issue.)

The format is ridiculously simple (always a plus); sit in a circle, take off your shoes, put on a blindfold (or just keep your eyes closed), throw your shoes into the center area, wait for the instructor to make sure all the footwear is well mixed, then try to find and put on your shoes. Time the attempt from start to the final shoe lace bow or loafer slip-on, so that the group will have an established record to try and better the next time. Timing an event always gives you (the instructor) an excuse for asking the group to try the task "one more time."

I was admittedly surprised at how enthusiastically the participants shed and rummaged through their shoes, considering the unspoken feeling that shoes were unclean and olfactorally associated with the owner. But rummage they did, and with alacrity, 'til all were reshod, smiling, and ready for more — more of whatever else you have to surprise and delight them with. *Barnyard?*

**Sharing Shoes**

I don't know what it is about taking shoes off and using them as game implements (foot fetish perhaps) but people like to do it, so here's another game which involves taking off that article of your clothing. If you think about it, shoes are the only article of clothing that we regularly wear of which there are two, so don't try to substitute other articles of clothing and explain to off-the-wall parents that... "It was Karl's idea."

- Take both shoes off or have someone else take them off — gnarly!

- Throw both shoes into a center pile. (This game does not work very well if only two or three people are playing — the more the merrier.)

- Find one of your shoes and one that belongs to someone else. (Do not play this game blindfolded or you will miss dinner and probably your next birthday.)

- Put yours on and find that special someone who belongs to the second shoe; your Cinderella, so to speak — gender notwithstanding.

- Share names and something personal, (number of children, shoe size, why they are at this particular workshop).

- Ask the group to get back together in a seated circle after allowing five minutes or so for this sharing. Have the couples (if a troika results, 's OK) introduce one another and relate what they have been told by their partner(s); much like the get-to-know-you scenario that takes place after the game Hog Call, (*Silver Bullets*, page 98).

## Shipwreck

I have been messing around with the basic "Shipwreck" game for years, but a letter from David Joseph (Essex, MA) indicated how much more detailed and fun this activity for younger students could be. The following is David's game set-up, quoted almost verbatim from his letter.

Using four markers (cones, coats, frisbees, etc.), outline a large square area or use one half a basketball court. Put about 25 kids into this square. Assign each side of the square as follows: Front — Bow; Rear — Stern; Left — Port; Right — Starboard. (Ed. Note: These designations are all relative to where YOU are standing and where you want the Front, etc., to be.)

As the captain of the vessel, your "crew" must do as they are told, or be:

- thrown overboard to the sharks
- walk the plank          } *(Ed. Note: — setting the tone)*
- eat the captain's cooking

Here's what the students must do as quickly as possible and in response to your commands.

- **Jellyfish** — ...on your back, with arms and legs jiggling in the air.

- **Sunbathing** — ...lying on your side.

- **Fish for Dinner** — ...jump up and down, holding your nose.

- **Can I Go to the Bathroom, Sir?** — Jump up and down, with legs crossed, while saluting.

- **Dig for Treasure** — Digging movements. (Sound effects are encouraged.)

- **Scrub the Deck** — ...on hands and knees, of course.

- **Mid Ship** — ...belly down in the middle of the ship. This is particularly funny when used in rapid alternation with

- **Jellyfish** and **Sunbathing**.

- **Crow's Nest** — ...on one knee, with a spyglass.

- **Bow** — Run to the bow of the boat.

- **Stern** — Run to the stern of the boat.

- **Starboard and Port** — Same as above.

- **Bow on Fire** — Run to the opposite side of the boat. Same for Stern, Starboard and Port.

The following commands are to be acted on and accomplished with a partner. It is important to emphasize the need for speed, so that the person next to you (male or female) responds to the joint need for a partner.

- **Man Overboard** — Piggy-back position

- **Man the Torpedoes** — Wheelbarrow position

- **Under Attack** — One person lies across (perpendicular) the other person's back.

- **Time for Grub** — One person represents a table (on all fours) and the second person sits gently on their partner's back while "eating."

- **Three Men in a Lifeboat** — Three people sit on the floor, one behind the other (like a toboggan) and row together singing a rowing song, "Row, row, row your boat..."

- **Shipwreck** — Everyone freeze!

As captain of the ship, you yell the above commands to your crew. Four or five commands in a row provides a functional and enjoyable challenge.

At the end of each group of commands, the last person to obey is OUT. Shipwreck can also be played non-competitively (no elimination), just for fun. Either way seems enjoyable to the kids and, as with most Project Adventure games, the more setting you create and enthusiasm you exude as captain, the more fun will be had by all.

### Speedy Gonzales

Did you enjoy playing Italian Golf? (*Bottomless Bag*, pg. 100). If so, you will like this speedy Mexican version. If you didn't like Italian Golf or don't know what I'm writing about, try it anyway.

The throwable object of play is the same one used in Italian Golf, the pessary passer, also called a deck tennis ring — it's a rubber donut-shaped ring that's fun to throw and catch and doesn't cause pain when an errant throw smacks you up-a-side the head. Pass the ring around a bit, getting used to the proper catching technique: fingers brought together in a spear configuration so that the thrown ring encircles the hand and passes over the wrist.

Here's the game.  Get together with three other players to form a "rapido" (that's Latin vernacular for a troika).  Then decide on a course that your team (your rapido) must navigate; like deciding on a "hole" in Italian Golf.  For example, from your starting position the rapido must travel (via the thrown rubber ring) around a tree, over a fence, in and out of a building, over the roof of a building, etc., etc.  In transit, the members of the rapido must pass the deck tennis ring from one member to another in a throwing sequence, and continue following that sequence.  Italian Golf required that the throws be well executed; in Gonzales Golf, both accuracy and speed are required.

The play object is to get around the chosen course in **the least amount of time,** while following these rules:

1.  Each player must carry a plastic gym spot marker, and stand on that gym spot each time the rubber ring is thrown.  This is to prevent players from throwing, missing, and then changing their throwing position to make the next throw easier.  The catcher must also carry and stand on a gym spot preliminary to each catch.  The catcher is allowed to leave the spot to catch the ring after the throw is in the air, but if the throw is errant or the ring is missed, the catcher must return to the spot and wait there for the next throw.

2.  There is no score kept for the number of throws, only elapsed time for completion of the course is recorded and compared.

3.  Throws must follow a decided upon, person-to-person sequence.  To complete a throw, the ring must be spear-handed, as in Italian Golf.

4.  If the ring is missed, it must be thrown again by the same person from the same plastic gym spot.  There are no penalties for missing a throw other than loss of time.

5.  Running between throws is not only necessary, but must be accomplished in a coordinated leap-frog fashion if a good overall team time is expected.  If your team is really laid-back and doesn't give a hoot about personal bests, competitive stuff, or the movie *Rocky*, introduce them to that low-prop favorite; existential golf, where each player is the mental architect of their own "hole."  Sitting comfortably in the shade, each player conceptualizes his/her own best round and then reports it to their teammates.  Some really fine scores have been recorded at this cognitive non-competitive level.

6.  Each rapido covers the same route. All teams start at the same place at the same time. Golf rules of etiquette are obviously not de rigueur.

    Play continues, *con mucho gusto,* until all the teams have established a time for the course. Then, after having interfaced, dialogued and argued about the various throwing, catching, and running decisions, another en masse round is attempted as before, so that each team has the opportunity to better their own best time, but also be *el campion de* Speedy Gonzales *por todo el mundo*, or at least for their school.

*Dos y dos son quatro y quatro y dos son seis. Seis y dos son ocho y ocho deis y seis. Y ocho veinte quatro y ocho treinte dos; Karlos va la escuela y tambien voy yo.*

The above bit of rhyming arithmetic via Español was included for those of you who remember Senorita Rodriquez on educational TV in the mid-60's. *"Buenas dias clase." "Buenos dias, Senorita Rodriquez."* I used to love the way she said "peanuts" in Spanish. Find a bilingual friend who can say peanuts in Español — it'll be one of your favorite words, too.

## DOTS

You ever play **DOTS** when you were a kid? Did you ever play **DOTS** as a parent, cause your kids badgered to you play? Your answer is probably, "**DOTS** is a hard game to avoid." If you don't remember the game, look at the grid of 16 dots below.

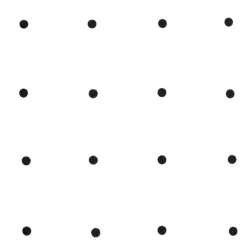

The object is to make a line between dots (alternating turns) until the line you make completes a square. You then get to put your initials in the completed square designating it as yours. The game continues apace until

7

all the dots have been connected. The person with the greatest number of personalized squares wins and gains bragging rights until the next grid war. It's an OK game for a rainy day if played once and maybe twice (depends on how hard it's raining), but beyond that, check out the following DOT game variations that actually require some thought and strategic machinations. Another plus is that these gridlock games can be played by small groups — often referred to as teams by Little League parents and hard core physical educators.

**DOT Variation #1** — Take turns. (See, we're cooperating already.) Mark any dot on your turn with either an X or O. Whoever marks four dots that make up a square, wins. The winner, to rub it in, outlines the designated square with the wildest color felt-tipped pen that s/he can find, while quietly remarking, "I sure do play this game well."

**DOT Variation #2** — Take turns. (No use dropping a good thing.) Link any two dots that are next to one another — up, down, sideways. Only one dot-to-dot line per turn, no more. The winner is the one who makes the last mark; i.e., the last line between dots. The person who is about to come in second **knows** it's going to happen, underlining the agony of defeat.

**DOT Variation #2-1/2** — (This variation isn't quite strong enough to get a whole number.) Take turns. You may draw a line of any length across, up, down, or diagonally. Make sure the line is from dot-to-dot within the grid, if you want to play the game, otherwise the line can go anywhere your marker goes. This variation is called Dot Travesty. You may not cross another line or turn a corner; straight lines only. The winner is whoever draws the last possible line.

If you were one of the existential game players that were drawing random lines of any length, up, down, etc., a curious game factoid is that drawing a squiggly line to Uranus would take longer than a fairly straight line to Pluto: esoteric info for advanced games people only, but I thought you plebeian players might be interested nonetheless.

## Fun With Nothing

I think this game will appeal to those of you with a low or nonexistent budget. *Fun With Nothing* was benignly plagiarized from Sarah Smeltzer, Pine Lake Environmental Center, Hartwick College, Oneonta, NY. She writes, "Stand in a circle with everyone mute. The leader mimes an object with a characteristic shape and weight, then explains that the object will be passed around the circle twice.

When received, each person can change the object any way they want without talking. This is an effective exercise in adapting ideas, non-verbal communication, creative thinking, and initiative."

8

I suspect the final object won't look much like what the initiator had in mind, but therein lies the fun.

## Bloody Hoopless

Sitting on the sunny playing field at Pennant Hills Scout Camp in Sydney, I was musing about the various adaptations applied to Moon Ball, and unexpectedly thought of another. I soon thereafter told Nancy MacPhee (national PA trainer working with me at the time in Australia) about the variation and then promptly forgot the whole thing.

Just recently, on another trip to OZ, I was reminded of my sunny inspiration by Jerry Barnes, an employee at Pennant Hills, and recently an intern at PA. Apparently, Nancy had introduced the game at a workshop while she and I were working at different venues, and Jerry had applied an Aussie name to it. I was asked why I hadn't written up the rules for inclusion in *BOT's*, and had to admit that I had forgotten about the game: I even had to be reminded of the rules. Enough soul-baring... here are the current rules as played by Telecom employees in New South Wales; with a few changes, of course.

Scratch marks in the dirt or place sections of retired rope on the ground to form a playing quadrant. Make the scratch lines or sections of rope at least 30' long, measured from the center of the quadrant.

Divide the group into four, more or less equal teams. Each team claims, then occupies a quadrant. Don't hesitate to play this game with large groups — lots of area and lots of action for lots of people.

Start play by whacking the Moon Ball straight up while standing near the center of the playing quadrant. (You whack it good the first time to demonstrate that wimpy hits are bogus, and to further display your beach ball prowess.)

Whichever quadrant the ball comes down in begins play. If the ball descends on or near a line, whichever team hits it first gets priority; open-hand hits only. The team with possession must hit the ball through a hand-held hula hoop before the ball can be smacked toward another quadrant. A team can hit the ball as many times as they want in their quadrant, but no one can hit the ball twice in succession. If the team in the receiving quadrant allows the ball to touch the ground, they lose a point. Remember that the only out-of-bound markers are the quadrant lines. Yes, these four lines extend to infinity. (Ed. note: There is no way to gain points, so Bloody Hoopless is obviously a low scoring game. No one actually loses, but no one wins big either. Ultimately, it's all in your point of view... Am I the world's tallest midget or the world's shortest giant? What's that got to do with anything...? I'm thinking...keep reading.

A few considerations:

- After the ball passes through the hoop, it cannot be hit toward another quadrant at a downward angle; i.e., no spiking. This rule must be strictly enforced, or teams will start to think about winning.

- After a "score," the ball is taken to the center and struck hard and high toward one of the other quads. If the ball comes down in the served quad, it must be struck again.

- If a team is scored negatively against, they must give up their hoop, (just lay it on the ground). To retrieve the hoop and their negative scoring ability, the team (when they next receive the ball in their quad) must hit the ball from person-to-person until everyone has made contact with the ball. Teachers and sociologists particularly like this sequence strike requirement, which is often referred to as the play-or-else rule.

- The game continues until either (1) You run out of balls (2) Someone announces morning tea or (3) Insidious ennui sets in, at which juncture someone flatly states, "Game over, man,"...and it is.

## Silly Veggies

Eric Schusser, from Dunstan High School in New Zealand, spent some time as an intern with Project Adventure a couple years ago, and he occasionally writes of his attempts to incorporate adventure programming into his teaching.

Eric uses the following game to break some ice and cause physical discomfort from excessive laughter. He writes: "A vegetable game for people who like to be silly, or a silly game for people who like to be vegetables."

The rules are as follows. (This looks an awful lot like a game I played in college that had to do with sucking down an inordinate amount of beer, but I know that a conscientious Kiwi like you wouldn't be involved with any malted beverage that smacked of hops and lager, eh Eric?)

1. Each person in a group picks a vegetable. Each person must be a different vegetable; twin tomatoes are out.

2. Ask each person to verbally announce his/her vegetable type. Do this two or three times. If any duplicates show up, ask one of the players to pick another veggie.

3. Starting with a volunteer (you pick one), that person must say his own vegetable name twice, followed by the name of

someone else's veggie twice. To inject some challenge into this simplistic requirement, each person must say both names with her lips totally covering her teeth and without smiling. Lips should be drawn tightly over the teeth.

If you show any sign of your pearly whites or crack a smile, **YOU'RE OUT OF THE GAME.**

The game continues with the next person saying the name of his vegetable twice and someone else's twice, etc., etc.

4.  If you mistakenly say the name of a veggie that has been removed from the game, then you also are summarily removed.

5.  Only facial contortions are allowed as harassment to the beleaguered veggies remaining. No talking or touching allowed.

6.  The game continues apace until only one person is left, or until everyone is sick of veggies and obviously ready for a round of Hog Call or Barn Yard.

**Quick Line-Up**

Use this run-around, willy-nilly activity to break some ice and provide a low-risk, low-skill sense of team affiliation.

First, however, you have to get the group to split themselves into four approximately equal groups. (Not to wander from the subject, but as I was sitting here six-finger tapping the old Tandy Laptop, I wondered why the word ABBREVIATION is so loong. How do you abbreviate the word abbreviation; a five syllable word? I started thinking about shortening words as I tapped out APPROXIMATELY above. Just a thought to share.) Quad grouping is easily accomplished by having everyone line up and then counting off 1-2-3-4, 1-2-3-4, etc. If that sounds like fun, you need help. Try this.

Ask each person in the group to pick which number (1-4) that they would like to be, but not to say or indicate what that number is. To discover which other participants were sharing your Zen and number, walk up to someone and shake their hand the number of times representing the 1-4 number that you mentally chose. If your number is 2 and someone tries to shake your hand 3 times, excuse yourself politely and continue your search. When you find a hand moving up and down congruently with yours, and if that hand stops at the appropriate number (jives with your karma), keep that soul buddy with you and, operating as a harmonic diad, try to find another free spirit vibrating on your joint frequency. Continue linking until everyone has established their affiliation with a numerical group. If you are lucky, the groups will be approx. (note the abbr. of approx.) equal in number. If not, ask a few noncommitted people to change groups to equal things up: I didn't say this grouping ploy worked perfectly. Be loose, be flexible. People usually don't care what group they are in, as long as they are having fun.

Now here's your role. Stand in the middle (a bit off-center is OK) of the gym or field and hold out both your arms so that your hands are pointing east and west. If you don't know which direction is east and west, any which way is fine, just so that you are pointing in opposite directions. Ask the four groups to orient themselves around you so that group 1 is north, group 2 is east, group 3 is south, and group 4 is west. Having groups orient themselves as to the points of the compass is interesting and entertaining, but, most significantly, causes strangers to have to talk to one another and share ideas and opinions. However, if you are pressed for time or compass headings give you a headache, just ask the four groups to arrange themselves equally around where you are standing. Whichever position they pick must become part of the group's memory, because as you move and reorient yourself as to the compass points or geographically in another part of the room/field, the groups, at your shouted signal of "DO IT" must all run to reorient themselves around you exactly as they were before you moved. The last group to achieve their proper position loses, and the three other groups get to hoot and howl and point fingers. There is no way to win this game, only lose, and losing in this context is not so bad, so who cares?

Make your first couple of moves simple; north to south, east to west type of thing. Then run to another part of the room before you shout DO IT, or stand on your head, or stand next to a pool...Continue to play until you have achieved some ice-breaking, or you notice that the level of enjoyment needs more joy.

**Trust Circle**

Don't present this activity until you are sure that your students care enough about one another to make it work.

Ask the students to arrange themselves in a circle. Announce, "Eyes closed and bumpers up." (Bumpers up is a hands-up, palms-out, elbows-in position that blindfolded or eyes-closed participants assume to protect their faces and bodies as they move slowly amongst one another.) Indicate that each person is going to walk slowly from one side of the circle to the other side and that everyone is to do this simultaneously. Obviously, there will be some jostling near the center of the circle, but if everyone is aware of the mass group movement, the shoulder bumps and palm contact should be no problem. If everything goes well, ask them to make another trip across the circle, but at a slightly higher rate of walking. More speed, more contact. Stress compassion for each other and ask for a willingness to protect one another from the consequences of uncaring contact. Ask for one more trip across the circle at a faster rate, **if** the group has handled the first two crossings in a desired fashion.

The purpose of this apparent disaster-waiting-to-happen is to promote caring between participants by including each of them in an activity punctuated with possible consequence. The safety of this activity is entirely dependent upon your "reading" of the group's readiness for controlled participation.

**DO NOT** use this activity if the group has not worked together toward developing a sense of caring for one another. If there is any fooling around, someone will get hurt, and the trust that you are trying to develop will diminish.

### Monarch

This game is written up in one of the *New Games* books, but I don't have one right here to copy from, so you are going to have to put up with my version of the activity. Actually, it's Steve Butler's version, because I learned the rules from him and have watched him present the game any number of times. Not a bad game all-in-all, if you don't make the mistake of using a red playground ball in place of a Nerf-type ball. Boundaries are variable as to the size of your group, but allow a goodly amount of running room.

The Monarch (the person IT) starts off with a dense, foam throwable (symbol of the monarchy) in hand. Choose the Monarch however you please, but don't pick the slowest, dead-armed thrower to start. The assigned Monarch tries to hit an anarchist (any other player) with the ball, at which juncture the just-hit anarchist becomes a joint Monarch. The two Monarchs then try to work together to hit another anarchist, etc., etc.

Include two balls (two monarchs) at the start of the game if the group numbers more than 20 players.

### *Rules:*

1.  If an anarchist runs out of bounds, s/he automatically becomes a Monarch.

2.  Monarchs cannot run if they have the ball in their possession. The ball can be passed to another Monarch, however.

The game continues until all the anarchists have been convinced to change their political affiliation by being hit with the ball — head shots do not count.

Monarch is kind of a no-boundary, bombardment type game and can be a disaster if you use a ball that no one wants to be hit by. Pat Kemp (subscriber) wrote recently, saying that she allows the kids to play a variation of Bombardment called *Cross Over Dodgeball*. She writes, "When hit, a player moves to the other team, thus eliminating the need to eliminate. Also, those who need the most practice at throwing and dodging aren't instantly knocked out of the game. The team with the most players after a specified time or the team with eventually everyone on it — WINS!" Pat emphasized that she uses only Nerf-type balls for these whackum-smackum games.

## Moonball Space Warp

Steve Butler showed me this useful variation of Moonball. See *Bottomless Bag,* page 55, for a review of the basic game.

For a group of 15-20 people, you will need one 20" beachball and two or three hula hoops. The object is to score as many ball strikes (points) as possible, with the scoring and rules set up in the following way.

### *Rules:*

1. One point is scored for each strike of the ball.

2. Two points are scored for a foot strike.

3. The score for each strike is doubled if the ball goes through a hoop after the strike.

4. The ball can only go through the hoop in one direction; i.e., it cannot be hit back and forth.

5. After a score is recorded, the hoop must be given to another player before another score can be made.

6. Hoops cannot touch one another; i.e., two hoops cannot be held together by one player.

7. If the ball hits the floor, the score returns to zero.

People are fascinated by gimmicks and high-tech gear that purport to make a task easier. Within the format of *Moonball Space Warp,* the use of the hoops seems to offer a way to gain points quickly and more efficiently. What the participants don't take into consideration is that when you make a potentially useful piece of gear available, you must also set aside a chunk of time to learn how to utilize the new technology; a computer, for example. But, everyone wants to use the new gear NOW, so ideas and notions are shouted and rejected as the players deal with the inevitable trial-and-error that results. It probably won't be noticed until later, because of the frenetic attempts at scoring points, but the hoops prove to be more of a hindrance than a help. If this realization is understood and implemented into future initiative attempts, something valuable has been learned.

**The Bottom Line**

This highly active one-group-game was initiated serendipitously at Pennant Hills Scout Camp, near Sydney, Australia in April 1989. The initial "bottom line" was a parallel pair of no-power lines that drooped usefully across our activity area.

*Objective:*

To hit a Space Ball (Moon Ball) over a horizontally-suspended section of bungee cord (1/4" diameter) ten times, without letting the ball hit the ground.

*Rules:*

- Everyone is on the same team.

- Each player can situate themselves wherever they or the team thinks they can best serve the objective.

- The ball can be hit as many times as desired before a scoring shot is attempted, but cannot be hit twice in a row by the same person.

- If the ball hits the ground, all accumulated scoring hits are discounted.

- The horizontal bungee cord should be at least 15' high, and no more than 18'.

- Catching or directing the ball is not allowed, however the ball can be struck, smacked, or kicked with any part of the body.

- The "beach ball" used as the play object should be 16" inches in diameter when inflated: plus or minus 2" is allowed within official NCAA **Bottom Line** rules.

- Comparing final scores with other on-site impromptu teams is inappropriate and generally frowned upon; however, attempting to reach a nebulous world record set by another equally nebulous team is approved of and encouraged by the ruling body.

- In keeping with the *Challenge By Choice* credo, whatever result a team is genuinely pleased with shall be accepted by the facilitator as a proper and fairly set world's record for THAT team, on THAT site, right THERE, right NOW. Such records are traditionally never recorded and seldom referred to beyond a fortnight.

## Considerations:

- String another section of bungee cord parallel to and 30" below the top bungee. If the ball is hit through this "window," two points are scored.

- If the wind is blowing, choose another initiative problem.

## Go To

Pure simple, pure fun. Use this game with grades 6-8, as suggested by Mike Browne at the Solomon-Lewenberg Middle School in Mattapan, MA.

Cluster a student group in the center of the gym and tell them that you are going to declare a destination, and that each person is to move to that geographical spot as quickly as possible. Have in mind a number of obvious and not-so-obvious destinations and verbally deliver them in such a way that the students don't have time to catch their breath or wonder why they are having such a good time doing something that has no tangible purpose. Remember the acronym F.U.N.N. (Functional Understanding's Not Necessary); that's why, if you need a reason.

Call out "Free throw line," or "Plumb line below the clock," or "Mr. Browne's whistle," or whatever seems challenging, fun, and within reason (your reason).

Notice that no mention has been made of teams, prizes, or winning. This game is for play only. Don't mention it.

## Acronyms & Initialisms

Print these acronyms and initialisms on 3"x 5" cards; one per card. Make a duplicate set of copies. Use a different color for the second set of cards. Hand out the cards to two equal groups and give them 15 minutes to come up with as many correct answers as possible. Be liberal with what's considered correct.

The team with the most right answers is ostensibly the winner, but obviously winning and losing is not the most valuable or significant part of this exercise. Ask the students to share the techniques that they tried and found to be most successful toward efficient use of the team's resources. The level of communication and cooperation displayed amongst participants should be represented (and pointed out) by the efficient gathering of correct answers. Playing one group off the other establishes an incentive to perform at a higher level, but team competition can be entirely eliminated (if not considered appropriate) by simply offering all the cards to one large group.

Most people are drawn to acronyms and abbreviations because they are used so often in day-to-day dialogue and communication. We often use an acronym knowing what it stands for, but remain ignorant as to what the individual letters represent — RADAR, for example. People are fascinated by what they don't know about what they think they should know.

ACRONYM — A Contrived Reduction of Nomenclature Yielding  Mnemonics

A&P — Atlantic & Pacific

AAHPERD — American Alliance of Health, Physical Education, Recreation & Dance

AARP — American Association of Retired Persons

AC/DC — Alternating Current/Direct Current

ACLU — American Civil Liberties Union

AD — Anno Domini

aka — Also Known As

AKC — American Kennel Club

AM — Amplitude Modulation, also Ante Meridiem

AMA — American Medical Association

APB — All Points Bulletin

ASA — American Standards Association

ASAP — As Soon As Possible

ASPCA — American Society for the Prevention of Cruelty to Animals

BART — Bay Area Rapid Transit

BBB — Better Business Bureau

BCD — Buoyancy Control Device

BMW — Bavarian Motor Works

CARE — Cooperative for American Relief Everywhere

CAT Scan — Computerized Axial Tomography

CCCP — U.S.S.R.

CD — Certificate of Deposit or Compact Disc

CEO — Chief Executive Officer

CHP — California Highway Patrol

CIA — Central Intelligence Agency

CNN — Cable News Network

CO — Commanding Officer

COLA — Cost of Living Adjustment

CPI — Consumer Price Index

CPR — Cardio-Pulmonary Resuscitation

DH — Designated Hitter

DINK — Double Income No Kids

DNA — Deoxy-nucleic Acid

DOA — Dead On Arrival

EEG — Electroencephalogram

EPA — Environmental Protection Agency

ESP — Extra-Sensory Perception

ETA — Estimated Time of Arrival

FDIC — Federal Deposit Insurance Corporation

FICA — Federal Insurance Compensation Act

FUBAR — Fouled Up Beyond All Recognition

FX — Special Effects

FY — Fiscal Year

FYI — For Your Information

GI — Government Issue

GORP — Good Ole Raisins and Peanuts

HBO — Home Box Office

HMO — Health Maintenance Organization

HUD — Housing and Urban Development

i.e. — id. est. (Latin for that is)

IBM — International Business Machine

ICBM — Inter-Continental Ballistic Missile

IRA — Individual (Invested) Retirement Account, or Irish Republican Army

KP — Kitchen Police

LASER — Light Amplification by Simulated Emission of Radiation

LAX — Los Angeles International Airport

LCD — Liquid Crystal Display

LED — Light Emitting Diode

LSD — Lysergic Acid Diethylamide

MADD — Mothers Against Drunk Drivers

MASH — Mobile Army Surgical Hospital

MGM — Metro-Goldwyn Mayer

MIA — Missing In Action

MO — Modus Operandi (Latin for Mode of Operation)

MOS — Military Occupational Specialty

NASA — National Aeronautics & Space Administration

NATO — North Atlantic Treaty Organization

NCAA — National Collegiate Athletic Association

NCR — National Cash Register

NOW — National Organization for Women

NRA — National Rifle Association

OHMS — On Her Majesty's Service

OPEC — Oil Producing Eastern Cartel or Organization of Petroleum Exporting Countries

PADI — Professional Association of Diving Instructors

PC — Personal Computer

PFD — Personal Flotation Device

pH — Potential of Hydrogen

PLO — Palestine Liberation Organization

PMS — Pre-Menstrual Syndrome

POSH — Port Out/Starboard Home

PS — Post Script

PST — Pacific Standard Time

PTL — Praise The Lord

QUASAR — Quasi Stellar Radio Source

R&D — Research and Development

R&R — Rest and Relaxation

RADAR — Radio Detecting and Ranging

RAM — Random Access Memory

RCA — Radio Corporation of America

REM — Rapid Eye Movement

RHIP — Rank Has Its Privileges

ROM — Read Only Memory

ROTC — Reserve Officer's Training Corps

RSVP — Respondez S'il Vous Plait

S&L — Savings & Loan

SAD — Seasonal Affective Disorder

SAE — Society of Automotive Engineers

SASE — Self-Addressed Stamped Envelope

SDI — Strategic Defense Initiative

SEAL — Sea Earth Air Land

SMOG — Smoke and Fog

SNAFU — Situation Normal All Fouled Up

SONAR — Sound Navigation Ranging

SOS — letters represent no words, but together designate a distress signal

SRO — Standing Room Only

STAT — Statim (Latin for hurry up)

STP — Special Treatment Product

SUNY — State University of New York

SWAT — Special Weapons and Tactics

TNT — Trinitrotoluene

TVA — Tennessee Valley Authority

TWA — Trans World Airlines

UDT — Underwater Demolition Team

UHF — Ultra-High Frequency

UIAA — Union of International Association of Alpinism

UNICEF — United Nations International Children's Emergency Fund

USFL — United States Football League

VCR — Video Cassette Recorder

VIP — Very Important Person

VISTA — Volunteers in Service to America

VP — Vice President

WAC — Women's Army Corps

WASP — White Anglo-Saxon Protestant

WAVES— Women Accepted for Volunteer Emergency Service

WHO — World Health Organization

YUPPIE — Young Urban Professional


## Bombouncement

The anti-game, Bombardment, has resulted in a love/hate relationship in schools throughout the world:  the kids love it, and the teachers hate it. That's not entirely true, because some of the inept students (designated targets) might choose not to "play," and a few toss-out-the-balls teachers use the game so they can read the paper, have a coffee, etc.

No matter how you look at it, the activity of trying to bash someone with a fairly hard ball to remove them from a game, lacks compassion and any measurable curriculum value.  (Reinforcing the skills of the skilled and re-emphasizing the limitations of the inept doesn't have much to do with curriculum value.  "Yeah, Bub, but we're talkin' real life here...if you can't cut it, get out of the kitchen — or something like that.")  I suspect many of the teachers reading this tongue-in-cheek condemnation would agree and could make a strong case against further use of Bombardment by any age or social group, but they continue to allow the game to be played because of "kid pressure" and tradition. You have to admit, the majority of kids love Bombardment and would rather pound each other with a red playground ball than shoot hoops. So, rather than eliminating the game, let's change a couple of the rules that militate against compassionate play and use the kids' enthusiasm for the throw-and-duck format to build acceptance for a superficially similar game, Bombouncement.

Bombouncement as a substitute for Bombardment was introduced to me by Kevin Corbett, who, also recognizing the negative values that were being reinforced by the physical mayhem and intimidation of Bombardment, began experimenting with minor rule changes (minor to the kids' conception of quality play, but major in the positive values being emphasized). Kevin said he was going to write up the game for me, but that was months ago, and deadlines have a way of sneaking up, so this is the way I remember hearing the rules defined.

Before I start rolling out the rules, let me relate a recent germane Far East observation. I was in Hong Kong about one hundred and thirty days ago, building a ropes course for the HK International School in Repulse Bay (a story in itself — great fun). Hong Kong's up-and-down topography being what it is, there is precious little flat space for much of anything, including playgrounds. So, at this multi-story high-rise school, the concrete playground is located on the 7th floor, and so was my apartment. Having been billeted so close to recess-land, I took advantage of the opportunity and spent some time watching the kids at play. (Not a bad way to pick up some ideas for NEW old games.) There were a couple ill-defined tag games going on, something that looked like soccer being practiced, considerable social chit-chat, and a few kids shooting hoops, but THE game that occupied the gweilos (white devils; i.e., Caucasians), Eurasians, blacks and Chinese, was a rounding, pounding session of bust-ass Bombardment. Not so hard to believe, I guess, considering the cosmopolitan range of students at the school. So, Hong Kong, Ireland, Malaysia, Australia, New Jersey, etc., here's a skill-oriented minimum contact alternative to an international favorite.

The object of Bombardment is to throw a ball over a center line or dead zone in order to hit and eliminate someone on the other team. (Rules vary as to where the anatomical hit must occur, but total-body seems to be the universal target of choice.) Some teachers say, "Don't hit anyone in the head." I say, "You gotta be kidding."

A player is eliminated from the game when hit, unless he (not many girls play Bombardment) happens to be the biggest, loudest kid who shrieks intimidatingly, "You missed me by a mile, Creep-O." The game continues until one side completely eliminates the other side. Those players eliminated 15 minutes ago, by this time, have drifted off to other recess activities or have snuck back into the game.

There is usually more than one ball in play in order to keep the activity level high. This multi-ball situation often results in a classic wolf pack scenario finale. As ball contact attrition wears one team down, the other team, sensing the kill, becomes more aggressive and even temporarily works together until there is only one hapless player left, faced by 6-8 ball wielding, rocket-armed terminators. The final act is too brutal to depict, but every thrown ball had YOUR CROTCH marked on it. Remember?

Change of Pace: In Bombouncement, the throwers must try to eliminate players on the other side by bouncing the ball near an opposing player. That target player MUST try to catch the ball after it has bounced. If the ball is caught, the game continues without penalty or award. If the ball is missed, the fumbling player is temporarily eliminated and must stand out of bounds in a developing queue of "hit" players. As players from each side are eliminated, they can return to the game each time their team eliminates someone on the other team, as per their place in line. There is a nice balance of knowing you can eliminate someone, but also recognizing that if you are "knocked out," your team has a good chance of reinstating you.

If a player fails to try for a ball bounced within their grasp or if that player is hit below the waist on the first bounce, s/he is also eliminated. The emphasis, then, is to try and throw the ball hard, but not directly at a person. If you hit someone directly, even inadvertently, you are eliminated (as per the rules above). You have a much better chance of eliminating players by bouncing the ball to their left or right than bouncing the ball directly in front of them.

I know I am probably forgetting some of the details, but the above rules should allow you to change Bombardment around in such a way that the fun remains, but the painful ball strikes are eliminated. Be aware that the one-bounce rule will wear your balls out quickly because of the frequent ball/concrete contact. Better the balls than your crotch, eh?

**Team Cream**

I don't know if I should be telling you about this game because of its purely aggressive roots and because it smacks of gratuitous violence, however, I played it (developed it actually) a few months ago with a group of 8th graders and have to admit enjoying the mayhem. Be aware that this game is not for everyone, and can be injurious to just about every bone in your body if played with adrenaline-pumped 8th graders. I escaped with a couple bruises and a strained shoulder.

I mentioned game roots above. The predecessor for Team Cream is a well known playground pastime that's fairly unorganized and usually not authorized, and which I can't identify directly, because the game title is unacceptably stereotypical. The purpose of this non-game is for one of the participants (there are no teams and very few rules) to maintain possession

22

of the object-of-play (OOP) by attempting to run around within the nebulous boundaries. Once this person is knocked down (tackled), he/she must give up the OOP only to that person who takes it from him/her. (I'm writing he/she,and him/her, but females seldom play this game, at least I haven't seen any girls submit themselves to this kind of punishment.)

Whoever is lucky (?) enough to grab the OOP, then attempts to run around willy-nilly until someone (usually more than one) abruptly stops their progress and guides them unceremoniously to the ground, etc. etc.

I think kids like this game because of the me-against-the-world feeling, which alternates with the let's-get-'em-team emotion. I'm also pretty sure that young boys like it because adults don't. But youngsters have been pursuing this playground game for generations (didn't you?), so if you want to offer a rule or two that at least injects some goal orientation and feelings of camaraderie, here're the rules for **Team Cream**.

Outline a rectangular area on sand or grass to measure about 100' by 50'. DO NOT PLAY THIS GAME ON CONCRETE OR HOT TOP. In fact you're probably better off not playing this game at all, but... A Nerf football makes a good OOP, but use anything soft. Break up into teams of two, (or three or four if there are lots of players). The object is for one of the teams to run the OOP up and down the field as many times as possible before one of the other teams, or teams in combination, takes the OOP away and begins their own attempt. Mark the ends of the playing area with a length of rope or whatever you have. A point is scored for each time a team makes one full field run. Play does not stop at any time. If a team scores a point, they just keep running (passing, lateralling, kicking) until they score another point, or lose the OOP.

One of the finer rule refinements of Team Cream is that after a player is guided to the turf, that player is not required to give up the OOP; it must be taken from him.

If the game continues for more than 2-3 minutes, conditioning begins to tell. Most potentially aerobic games that are currently played, intersperse time slots of very intense physical activity with down times for sucking wind (usually called planning time or playmaking by out-of-breath wind suckers). A study recently showed that a pro football player spends approximately four minutes of aerobic activity during a sixty minute game. There is no "breathing" time while playing Team Cream, so half the players can usually be found lying on their backs wondering why the air is so thin on their particular part of the field. I consider myself in better then fair condition, but 5 minutes of flat-out Team Cream sent me to the sidelines looking for more lung space.

For the sake of your bodies, do not allow blocking of any kind, and certainly no blind-side, knee-high tackles. Don't take this game seriously, and you will have a much safer and enjoyable time. It's a fun game to play with the neighborhood kids on a fall afternoon. I don't think I'd want to "play" with a group of people my own size; particularly if they were serious about winning. I'm seldom serious about winning (except when I play Monopoly with my wife), so come play Team Cream over at my house some afternoon. Oh, and...uh, bring a cup... right, not for tea.

## Cone Soccer

Remember **Tree Soccer** (*Silver Bullets; page 68*). If you don't have trees in the right position, or any trees at all, put two cones out on the field of play and use the same rules that apply to Tree Soccer. Not a high scoring game, but ultimately aerobic.

## You Bet Your Buddy

An amusing, action betting game that generates feelings of excitement, rejection, teamwork, loyalty, and deception.

Teach the game Rock–Paper–Scissors to those in the group who have never played or forgot how; i.e., became too mature. Quick review — Rock (fist) breaks Scissors; Scissors (two fingers) cuts Paper; and Paper (flat hand) covers Rock.

Divide your group in half. (Here's a quick and innocuous 50/50 split technique. "Everyone fold your hands. If your right thumb is on top, you are in group A; if your left thumb is on top, team B is your alliance.")

Before getting together for the first team R-P-S confrontation, each team must huddle and decide what hand configuration their designated throwers (DT's) will show. Two sequences are chosen in case the first throw is a tie.

The game becomes more intense as the players decide which team members will represent pawns (chips) for the upcoming bets; i.e., bets as to which team will win the R-P-S showdown.

With the two DT's facing one another, that team with the most left-handed people gets to establish the first bet. For example, "Our team bets two pawns." (Two players on both sides, who at this point must disengage themselves from the groups and stand aside, as part of the "pot.") The other team must accept the bet, and is allowed to raise one pawn if they desire.

The R-P-S action ensues, determining a winner. The winning team receives the bet pawns from the other team. If the first throw is a tie, the betting team can (1) up the bet and continue, (2) withdraw to re-sequence, (3) continue. Pawns can switch roles after each winning sequence.

The game continues until one team "breaks the bank" of the other team: no more pawns to bet.

In the debrief session afterward, ask:

> How did you feel as a pawn?
>
> How did you feel toward the pawns?
>
> Did you always faithfully work for the team you were currently allied with, or did you remain faithful to your initial team?
>
> Did you always enjoy winning?
>
> Did you worry about losing?
>
> Would you have liked to be the DT?

## Minnesota Mosquito

Ron Ball writes that the Minnesota state bird is the mosquito and having, many years ago, experienced that state *bird* in some abundance at the Minnesota Outward Bound School (now the Voyageur OB School), I'd have to agree. Ron offers the following tag game based on this famous "bird."

Select one or two players to act as mosquitos, and equip each mosquito with an ethafoam sword (stingers). When a player is stung (no head hits) he/she is frozen, and remains so cryogenetically suspended until two unfrozen players encircle the afflicted player with their arms and shout, "DEEP WOODS OFF," or "DI-ETHYL META TOLUMIDE" before being stung themselves.

The players trying to keep from getting stung can band together in hand-in-hand groups of four (maximum) to try and surround the mosquito. When this is accomplished and the two outside players slap their hands together, WHACK... that's the end of the mosquito (scratch/scratch), and the game (scratch/scratch) until you start again.

## Rug Rats

Get yourself down to a rug store and ask if they sell rug samplers or rug remnants. These rug sections measure about 14" x 18" and have a finished edge. I think the salesmen keep them around to show buyers what a particular type of rug looks and feels like. I bought 20 of these sections recently for $.75 apiece.

Here's what to do with your newly purchased (donated?) rug sections.

1.  In a gymnasium, collect your group at one end of the basketball court; give them the rug sections; announce

that the floor is covered with sole acid (dissolves the bottom of the shoes); and ask them to make it to the other end of the court in the quickest, most efficient way. I don't have to list solutions here because the group will soon come up with at least one. Remember to announce that if anyone steps off a rug section, they must return to the start and begin again.

2.    If someone uses the rug sections as floor skates, everyone will soon realize that this is the quickest and most efficient way to get around and have the most fun on the floor. Put the nap to the floor for the best movement. This technique only works on a polished wood or stainless steel floor.

3.    After the group has accomplished their goal of getting across the gym floor, set up some Olympic rug skating races. Suggest tandem races, also. I have personally timed a rug-skate-gym-crossing in just over 6 seconds. We're talking quality performance here!

## Just Lying Around

As a chosen article is passed from person to person, each player makes up a fanciful story (lie) about the object. The enjoyment comes from listening to the various tall tales.

Of course, each person is allowed to pass if they so choose. Include a final vote for the best/worst lie, most entertaining, shortest, etc., etc.

Choose interesting objects in order to spark the creative imagination of your players. This activity is best introduced well into the program; i.e., when the students begin to respond to spontaneously presented curriculum and also have developed a level of trust with one another.

## I'm Thumbody

This variation is an original, obtained from Bruce Waguespack, Baton Rouge, LA. Bruce suggests using the activity to break some ice at the beginning of an activity or workshop session. Have lots of ink pads available for the many fingerprints that will need recording.

The following grid page is reproduced almost entirely from the one Bruce sent along, and I believe explains itself. I suspect that the parenthetical KEEP IT's refer to a time span commensurate with the game and not in a finders-keepers context. I'd like to think the KEEP IT command was included to build trust.

I think it would be fun to make up a grid yourself or at least supplement this one with activities that mirror your group's demographics and inclinations. Check the "Have you ever...?" 500 list in *The Bottomless Bag* (starting on page 142) to get some ideas.

The winner(s) are those who enjoy themselves the most — on a scale of one to eleven...unless it's REALLY fun and then you can spring for twelve.

Get as many different thumbprints as you can, one in each square. You **MUST** do each activity before you get their thumbprint.

## I'm Thumbody

| Someone with red or green underwear. | Untie someone's shoe, tie it back. | Get a watch from someone (keep it). | Some with their birthday in the same month as yours. |
|---|---|---|---|
| Get a driver's license from someone (keep it). | Someone who's more bald than not. | Get two people to hug each other. | Someone with braces. |
| Someone who smiles a lot. | Get a shoestring from someone (keep it). | Someone who needs a haircut. | Someone who can sing (they must sing at least one verse of a well known song). |
| Someone with wrist or ankle jewelry. | Someone with designer jeans on. | Someone with blond hair. | Someone with glasses. |

## Body Sac

There's something about the game Hackey Sac that makes me uncomfortable. I suspect part of the reason is that I don't kick the sac very well, and being quickly identified as a quick-twitch/no-contact kicker, a high functioning footy group that is trying to establish a "world record" gives off palpable "you can play, but..." vibes that rattle the maladroit ego and elicit the quintessential cop-out comment: "This game sucks!" Well... it doesn't, as evidenced by the laid-back, *"Don't say you're sorry, man"* kicking circles that seem to appear whenever there isn't a basketball available. How come so popular? To wit, Hackey Sacs are easily transportable, necessary play space is minimal, the rules are super-simple, competition against self is de rigueur, and the eye/foot coordination necessary is transferrable to other games. Kicking the small seed bag around is fun, if not somewhat elitist, and therein, I think, lies the rub; the amount of time necessary to gain the requisite kicking skills to gain satisfaction often results in a round ball retreat. How about trying a game that allows the use of already practiced skills while the new ones are being brought up to satisfying snuff; i.e. satisfying to the player. Enter **Body Sac**, a recent full-body contact invention of me and Jose, plus a playful handful of folks from the annual OTRA (Oklahoma Therapeutic Ropes Association) Conference at Camp Redlands — about an hour's drive from Oklahoma City.

During a break, on the first day of the conference, I watched Jose maneuvering a regulation Hackey Sac around with an impressive level of below-the-waist skill, as he waited for the inevitable two or three other kickers that seem to appear whenever a scrunchy seed sac takes foot flight. I watched the foot, knee, ankle sequence for a couple minutes, then remembered a whimsical purchase I had made the week before at Child's World — I'm a toy store junkie. Searching and groping around inside my highly organized game bag, I eventually found the new purchase; a macro seed bag that looks just like a Hackey Sac, but is about three to four times as large. Manually flipping my *BIG* sac casually up and down, I ask Jose if he has ever played Hackey Hand? Intuitively (ego preservation) I had eliminated the crux of my intimidation; i.e., not being able to control the flight of a small object with my feet. Now we were going to play at (not *play at* a game, just play) keeping this comfortably sized object aloft by using hand contact only. Open hand whacks made more sense (to me) considering the size of the new seed sac, and the admonition on the packaging that stated unequivocally, "This play sac was not designed for kicking." There it was in black and white, a justification for developing a new game, and particularly since the sac came without any instructions (except what not to do).

Jose and I manually smacked the sac around a bit, suggesting to one another after a few hits that maybe we could keep score, which we did. But before we could set a standard, others were attracted to our gymnastic hits and saves and were, of course, immediately included within our non-elitist cadre of upright, prehensile, manually dexterous, sac-whackers.

Recognizing that this was a "new" sport being established, the suggestions for satisfying play came fast and furious from the hands-on participants. Here's what resulted from that intensely creative play period, on the friendly fields of Camp Redlands, Oklahoma — "...where the winds come whistling down the plains..."

- No points are scored if the sac is whacked manually. Hand hits are strictly utilitarian, used only to keep the sac aloft — off the ground.

- Points are scored as follows: one point for foot contact, three points for contact with any part of the body between the waist and the neck, (not to include the serve) and two points for cranial contact.

- After any scoring contact, the sac must be passed to another player before an additional score can be recorded. This pass can be made manually or otherwise.

- Only three manual hits are allowed per player, before the sac must be passed on or scored with. For example, a player can hit the sac three times, score, then hit the sac an additional three times.

- "Carrying" the sac to control its flight is not allowed.

I think the game was well received because: (1) The group made up their own rules. (2) The use of hands was allowed, to keep the game moving (as contrasts Hackey Sac, where misses and starting over are frequent and eventually tedious). (3) The entire body can be used innovatively to score points.

*Ed. Note: I have tried this game with a regulation Hackey Sac, and it plays almost as well.*

## Gully Gully

This one really baffled me, which isn't saying much, considering that I am easily baffled. Dick Bennett of the Painesville, Ohio YMCA showed me the procedure and the not-so-obvious answer.

### Objective

A volunteer thinks of a brief well known phrase, or the name of a famous person. The game facilitator (GF), through a series of apparently indecipherable sounds, sentences, and hand movements, indicates to an in-the-know compatriot who that famous person is. The object for the group is to determine how this communication is achieved.

To wit: The first letter of a sentence is taken as the letter to begin a word. For example, if the chosen famous person were Jesus, the facilitator would start a sentence (any sentence) with the letter J: *Just listen carefully*. If the next letter in the name is a vowel, which it is, the GF flashes fancy hand signs to indicate a number from 1-5, that is, a-e-i-o-u. In this case, two hand signs are flashed for the letter *e*. The letter *s* is indicated by the sentence, *Suppose we stop here*. The letter *u* receives 5 hand flashes. The final letter (sentence) is up to you. Suppose you can you handle it?

If you choose two names to communicate — say Ben Hur — the GF says *Gully Gully* to end a word. If two people have been working this game together for a long time, many words can be communicated. The seemingly nonsensical sentences, sounds and patterns that come so easily to the facilitator add to the perfect confusion of the audience. Just right for a campfire or a rainy day.

# Chapter Two
# *Initiative Problems*

## Grid Code

This brief offering doesn't have much to do with adventure programming, but... When I was a kid (late 40's, early 50's — that's 1940, 1950, not my age — although either way of thinking about it seems to fit:  your choice), I was always sending away for some cereal box decoding geegaw.  I loved the idea of sending and receiving secret messages, and if an attractive solid gold-plated gizmo was involved, so much the better.  I wish I had kept my collection of Captain Marvel, Little Orphan Annie, and Sky King decoders; seems like that type of thing is worth quite a bit now to collectors.  Makes you wonder, what inexpensive, gimmicky thing on the market now will be a valuable collectible 50 years from now.

Since I liked codes and secret messages way back when, I was taken by this logical, but hard-to-crack grid code.  If you have children, I think they will like it, too.  If you don't have kids, better borrow some, 'cause this code is fairly sophisticated for beginners.  The illustration pretty much explains the code mechanism, but...each code letter is represented by a diagram of the box it's in.  Dots are added to the diagram to indicate the proper grid.  Here's your magic message for this issue (check out the tic-tac-toe grid illustrations).  Look for future messages; same time, same place. "Plunk your magic twanger, Froggie."

Using the preceding letter grid, each letter is represented by a diagram of the box it is in, with a dot added for the second grid, and two dots for the third. So try this on for a message.

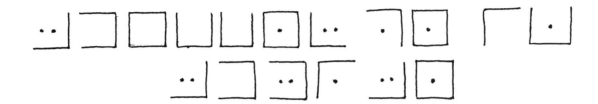

### Site/Central

The Executive Reach trainers at Project Adventure have been successfully using an initiative problem variation that they refer to as the Site-Central approach. This technique speaks to the management/field worker dichotomy that often develops in a white collar/blue collar work environment, where a small group of well-paid management workers regularly set policy and "manage" less well-paid workers who accomplish the hands-on tasks that result in producing a saleable product.

### *Management*

"If those lazy workers would ever get off their duffs and pay attention to our guidelines, maybe we could get something done around here."

### *Workers*

"If those lazy do-nothings in their ivory tower would ever listen to us maybe we could get something done around here."

The use of a Site-Central approach to problem solving can be occupationally and personally revealing to both work factions and thus helpful toward establishing a dialogue and understanding of the communication and trust dilemma that establishes this we/they schism as potentially the most complex and counterproductive personnel problem in today's business world.

You don't get it? Too much verbiage? Here's the straight scoop. If you know what I'm talking about, skip this remedial section.

The management (salaried coat and tie guys) think the workers (blue collar, hands-on, hourly wage guys) are lazy, uncommitted and basically boorish.

The workers think the management people are overpaid, out-of-touch, pompous BS'ers. Got it? Good.

Here's the way Site/Central works. Divide your team in thirds and designate one third as management (Central) and the other two-thirds as workers (task force). Place the workers at the site where you expect them to physically attempt to solve the initiative problem (whichever problem you have chosen). Place the management people in a room or somewhere distant from the solution site so that they cannot see or hear the workers.

### Rules:

1. A liaison person should be chosen from the management group. This person is allowed free passage from group to group at any time, and may talk freely with both groups. The liaison person is not affiliated with either group, but is part of the profit-sharing package and is therefore interested in the final product.

2. The workers can do nothing without explicit instructions or approval from Central. Work orders are passed along only by the liaison person. Workers can think and plan but are not allowed to implement without specific instructions to do so.

3. Central has an instruction sheet identical to the one the workers have. This sheet provides the scenario for the problem and lists the rules.

4. The liaison person is not allowed to write anything or pass along notes to either team. Only verbal communication between groups, via the liaison, is allowed.

### Debriefing Suggestions:

Have each team do a self-evaluation of their own process to be shared with the other team. Also have each team evaluate the other group. Finally, have each group make clear, concrete suggestions to themselves and the other group of what they might do differently (i.e., more effectively) the next time.

Things to look for when observing teams.

Organization, roles, use of time, degree of control of the workers by Central, interest of the worker's morale, efficient use of incoming information, clarity of communication, encouragement of innovation, visioning, relation with liaison, initiative, degree of commitment to task, attempt to influence Central, degree of support felt by workers.

Flip-flop teams during other initiative problem situations. Remember that using this technique is going to be more time consuming than doing an initiative with a single group. Either allow a sufficient amount of time for the inevitable communication exchanges and necessary debriefing dialogue or wait for another situation when sufficient time will be available. Site/Central is not a 30-minute time-filler: plan the activity, pick your sites beforehand and prepare significant comments and questions for the debrief session.

## The Square Route

I received this puzzle and related relay activity from Peter Steele (Fox Lane Middle School, Bedford, NY). Peter has been teaching a Project Adventure/ Outdoor Education combo for a number of years and is, not surprisingly, a very inventive guy. I changed your puzzle and rules just a bit, Peter — check it out. And...thanks.

"The object of this activity is for two teams to cross a mystical marsh area using only the six separate pieces of the puzzle as stepping stones. Puzzle sections must be used and transported across the marsh and then pieced together to form a perfect square." (I've never seen a square that varied much from perfection, unless it's squarish.)

The catch? No one can step backward more than once and no one can carry more than one "stepping stone" at a time. The first team to reach the other side of the marsh (30') and solve the problem, gets to use their sections to help the other team (which is really one big team, but I indicated two teams so that Little League parents would feel comfortable reading this).

During the marsh traverse, if a player steps or falls off a puzzle section, the entire "half team" must return to the starting position for another good ole try.

The puzzle, as depicted on the following page, measures 4' x 4' and is made of rug material or whatever else you can scrounge up for free. Scale: 1" = 1' or one inch = 12 meters. If you use the meter measurement scale (metric equivalency requirement), it will be necessary to allow the use of a forklift to solve this problem.

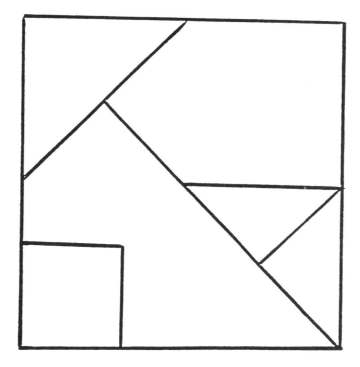

Puzzle measures 4' x 4' and is constructed from foam padding or rug material.

P.S.   You can do this activity as an initiative with a group and forget the relay aspect.

## Squash Ball

I'm just back (to New England) from a ropes course building/training trip overseas, and still a bit jet-lagged; to the extent that I'm waking up at odd hours wide-eyed and wired.  So, last night, when the wee hour wakies were throttling my Z's, I thought a thought and came up with this low prop initiative task that's fun and physically demanding.  My 2:47 a.m. name for the activity was "Bust My Balls," but at dawn I thought better of the parental consequences, and accepted the name suggested by Mike Downey — as above.  Here's the task.

*Individual* — Each person is offered four used (new is OK) tennis balls and a stout 6' pole. The object is to get from A to B (about 20 feet) using only these props and making no contact with the floor. The obvious (I think) solution is to step on the fuzzy spheres with the ball of your foot, and leaning on the pole for support, try to use the sequenced balls as "stepping stones" to your destination. Don't conceptualize it, try it.

*Group* — Each person gets four tennis balls, but only one pole per four people. Increase the travel distance to 30 feet. To dramatically increase the difficulty, don't offer the use of any poles. Try holding hands to increase a pair's stability.

Ann Smolowe, Project Adventure's Executive Reach Director, professional masseuse, and very pregnant lady (at this writing), said that walking on tennis balls stimulates many (I forget how many, but lots of) nerve endings in the foot that can positively affect other parts of the body, your body. So, get squashing...

## Traffic Jam — The Answer

People have asked me from time to time during workshops, "Do you know the series of sequence moves necessary to solve The Traffic Jam?" My answer has always been, "Yes... kind of," which means, if necessary I can work out the solution in a couple minutes — God knows, I've seen it done often enough. I never felt it was necessary to memorize the 24 moves needed to complete the problem, recognizing that a motivated group will inevitably come up with the solution anyway. Wallowing in ignorance also prevents me from feeling pedagogically obliged to give *just a little hint*. If the group is not motivated, and it becomes apparent that a solution is not forthcoming this day (week/month), just mention that the problem isn't going anywhere, and that it might be best to think about it for awhile (at least until tomorrow or until you can sit down and figure the darn thing out again).

However, if not knowing bugs you, and you want to write (tattoo) the solution on your thigh (lots of room there), here's the answer. Oh...wait...if you don't know what the problem is, the answer isn't going to do you much good, is it? Look on page 122 of the book *Silver Bullets* for the framing of this cerebral initiative problem. It's a useful task for the right group at the right time. Traffic Jam is not included in *The Bottomless Bag.*

Label the nine boxes from left to right according to the following diagram.

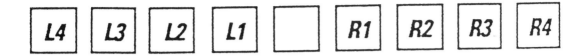

The people standing in the boxes should remember their R or L designations. If your players mix up their L's and R's, you and they will become very frustrated.

Here's the sequence that allows a solution. Remember that the players can only move around someone that they are facing and can never move backward.

L1, R1, R2, L1, L2, L3, R1, R2, R3, R4, L1, L2, L3, L4, R1, R2, R3, R4, L2, L3, L4, R3, R4, L4. This sequence indicates 24 distinct moves, no more, no less, and 24 it should be, as recordeth by the scribes that record such tedious things.

I enjoy hearing from people on the phone about ropes course construction concerns, or answering questions about certain game rules, and even occasionally discussing the intricacies of adventure philosophy, but you better not call me about The Traffic Jam...'cause I'm not in.

**Pinhole Picture**

Bill Oakley from Pennant Hills Scout Camp near Sydney, Australia, wrote a smallish pamphlet for the scouts a few years ago called, *USE YOUR INITIATIVE*. I was reading through it the other day looking for ideas to embellish (creative plagiarizing) and came upon the following activity, which I think has the makings for a useful group initiative problem. Not an altogether unusual situation actually, considering that Bill's booklet is entirely about initiative problems.

Make up a rectangular cardboard box, about the size of a shoe box. In one end, on-center punch a small hole (about 1/8" diameter). At the inside opposite end of the box, paste or tape a highly contrasted and detailed picture or photograph. Allow enough light to enter the box (cut louvers) so that when you look through the small hole (one eye), you can see the picture clearly.

Allow each person in the group to have a ten-second peek through the hole. After everyone has had their quick look, ask the group to reproduce (draw) the picture as they remember it and as accurately and detailed as possible.

Compare the group's reproduction with the original. Talk about the differences and similarities and why they occurred. Ask the group to look at another picture through the peekhole and try again to jointly (synergistically) draw what they see and remember. (Drawing is not allowed to begin until the last person has had his look.) See if the accuracy of the second attempt varies from the first.

Are different areas of the picture assigned to different peekers? Is the task assessed in an ongoing way? Does someone act as spokesperson or team leader?

## Nocturnal News

I haven't tried this unique nighttime initiative problem yet, but I know that it "works," from having talked with people who have wielded the flashlight and aimed the mirrors.

The object is to read an assigned paragraph from a newspaper sheet that has been tacked at about eye level onto the trunk of a tree. Not so hard, it would seem, until you consider that the reading must be accomplished in the dark. Grasping the nocturnal essence of the challenge, it's probably best to present this task at night.

Materials needed: one large flashlight (torch), three pocket (purse) mirrors, four thumb tacks, a sheet of newspaper print containing a lurid tabloid event of prurient interest.

The problem is presented so that the players realize the flashlight cannot be used to directly illuminate the news sheet. In fact, the light from the torch must be directed and redirected via the three mirrors before the light can be beamed onto the tacked sheet. Simply provide the materials (you tack up the news sheet), and say that they must relate the details (better not make the story too lurid) concerning the felt-tipped outlined story.

## *Rules:*

1. The torch cannot be taken in the 180 degree area on the newsprint side of the tree, nor can it be shined directly onto the newssheet.

2. Only one mirror is allowed into this 180 degree half-circle area.

3. The light must be reflected off all three mirrors before it illuminates the paper.

4. Five people are assigned to each torch team.

**The Quad Jam**

This simple variation of the TP Shuffle (*Bottomless Bag*, pgs. 243-244) was sent by Craig Dobkin of West Pines Psychiatric Hospital in Colorado. Craig also gave me a useful idea for small groups that involves traversing over and above and under a table...but that's a couple paragraphs below.

Do this...build a square on the ground using 4 – 4" x 4" x 8' boards. Use countersunk 1/2" x 6" galvanized lag screws to produce a solid joining of the boards. Place this squarish (everything I build has the *ish* appendaged on for obvious out-of-plumb reasons), structure on top of eight cinder blocks, so that the blocks are situated under the corners and sides of the structure. In case there's any doubt — place the blocks long-side on the ground; not on end. I knew you knew that. So situated, the 4 x 4 square will accommodate 20 standing people — 5 per board. If you have a larger group (30-50), use the elevated 4 x 4's as a spatial All Aboard.

As a warm-up activity, ask the balanced group to circle the square: perform a 360 degree circuit, obviously without stepping off the boards. See how fast a 360 degree circuit can be made. Considering that there are four teams (consisting of 5 on each board), ask groups 1 and 2 to switch boards and end up in exact order. Ask 3 & 4 to do the same. Try 2 & 4 and 1 & 3 for a switcheroo. Also insert the non-verbal "You're mute" trick for an additional challenge. Don't forget to spot on the outside of the square for those participants who look like they are going to need a catching hand.

**The Over/Under Pass**

I have to tell you right off that this table traverse is a genuine physical challenge for either an individual or a group. Make sure you do some stretching before attempting this demanding traverse.

Craig Dobkin of Boulder, CO, suggested this event as a group challenge (the illustration also came from Craig). I can remember spending some evening hours at NCOBS in the late 60's challenging each other with this type of thing, but never imagining that it would be an effective group task also. Well, it is, so take a look at the following description and give it a try. If you find the individual attempt too daunting, ask a friend if he/she would like traversing a table with you.

The illustration, although well done in a humorous sense, depicts a table that is much too flimsy to support multi-people. The positioning of the people doesn't engender much trust either, so use some spotting during head-down attempts. In order to maintain that fine balanced sense of marital *wa,* build your own table rather than trying to adapt someone's (you know who's) dinner table. Here are the dimensions of a hefty table that Dave Klim (PA builder) banged together a few months ago.

The four legs are made of treated (wolmanized) 4" x 4" x 33" boards. Two 4" x 4" x 30" boards are lag screwed to the tops of two of the 33" legs. Countersink the heads of the 1/2" x 6" lag screws. Nail two 2" x 12" x 6' boards and one 2" x 8" 6' board (not pressure treated) onto the 30' 4 x 4's. The completed table top measures 30" wide and 6' long.

Cut sections of 1/2" plywood (right triangles) to **screw** onto the corners of the table in order to add support. That's a total of 8 triangular sections. OK, there's your table. What are you going to do with it?

Ask 4-5 people to try and traverse the table in the direction indicated by the illustration. All 4-5 people start and finish the traverse on top of the table. To quote Craig, "The object is to get each participant, one at a time, under and back on top of the table without touching the ground. The illustration shows going head first, which is possible, but it's much easier to go sideways." Craig continues, "Some rules you might want to use:

- If a person touches the ground, they must return to the top of the table and begin again.

- Only the person going under can talk, and therefore they need to ask for whatever help they need.

- The person going under cannot use their arms or perhaps their legs or maybe even both, putting all the responsibility on their support system.

- Tape notes under the table to be shared with the group for a bit of humor."

To make this event as safe as possible, ask two spotters to support the table to prevent tipping. Assign spotters liberally to those people who seem to need their support.

*Note: The dimensions of the above table are arbitrary. Change the measurements as to the physical capabilities of whatever group you plan to be working with or alternately build a couple different sized tables to vary the challenge. Whatever size you end up with, make sure that the structure is strong enough to support the people you put on top. Look at the inverted fellow's head position in the cartoon. What do you think would happen to his neck if the table pancaked? Right!*

## Croc Pit

During a business sojourn to Australia, I spent some time training and working with company trainers from Telecom. (Telecom represents Australia's telecommunications industry.) During this pleasant and productive period, we shared various training and curriculum ideas. The "Croc Pit" is a *fair dinkum* example of an initiative problem that their trainers use often and effectively. Since returning to the U.S., I've watched some of the Project Adventure staff present the Croc Pit problem to various student groups. This well-received task results in a tough 45 to 90 minute initiative scenario. For a highly functioning group that has yet to be challenged, this physical and cognitive poser is a good choice.

Materials needed: Four 6' metal fence pickets (sturdy wooden 2"x 3" stakes are ok); approximately 75' of 3/16" diameter bungee cord; two plastic milk crates (the substantial kind); one 4"x 4"x 6' board; one 2"x 8"x 7'11" board; one 2"x 8"x 5' board.

Mark out a slightly out-of-square rectangular area on the ground (grass) that measures exactly 8' x 8'6". Drive one of the fence pickets into the ground at each corner. Tie a length of bungee cord around the rectangle's perimeter so that it measures (from the ground) two inches below the height of a milk crate. Tie a second parallel length of bungee cord around the staked out rectangle so that it measures 24" above the lower bungee cord. Your pounding and tying should produce some thing that looks like a miniature boxing ring; i.e., a smallish crocodile pit.

The completion object of this demanding initiative problem is to move your group from one side of the croc pit to the other side without (1) touching any of the bungee lengths or (2) touching the crocodile-infested interior of the rectangle (grass) — consequences listed below.

## Rules:

- No one is allowed to pass over the top bungee cords. (I don't think it could be done anyway.)

- No other props are allowed except those indicated; this includes articles of clothing.

- If anyone touches any bungee cord with anything, they must return and begin again.

- If a board touches the grass/ground inside the pit, that board must be returned to the start.

- If you want to increase the difficulty of the problem, request that the group finish up with all the props on the terminal side of the croc pit.

## Procedural Tips

Both 2 x 6 boards are measured so that they will not individually fit across the pit. If the long 2 x 6 is placed on a milk carton just outside the pit, a person can crawl between the two bungee cords and out onto the board so that the second milk carton can be placed outside the far side of the pit. This initial 2 x 6 board will not support the weight of a participant unless the 4 x 4 is placed onto and perpendicular to the end of this crate supported board. So placed, participants can add their weight (counterweight) by sitting on the 4 x 4, allowing a light/strong player to crawl to the end of the extended 2 x 6 and place the second milk crate to the far outside of the pit. The 5' board can then be placed on top of the end of the long board so that it reaches and rests on top of the far milk crate.

The obviously simple procedure then, is to have each participant crawl between the near bungee cords, across the boards and through the far cords to safety. This fairly tedious procedure is followed until the last couple of people are left and...the rest is up to you. You don't want me to tell you everything, do you?

Be ready to devote a considerable amount of time to this initiative problem. The discussion/trial-and-error segment may take 30-45 minutes. Efforts of well over an hour are not uncommon. It follows that this tough passage is more adaptable to a mature group that can maintain keen interest in successful completion, even when progress (physical and/or conceptual) slows. However, **any** fabricated initiative problem must have enough fantasy-challenge-fun to provide an ongoing sense of satisfaction or at least provide promise of completion.

**Sticky Wicket**

I picked up this variation of the Carabiner Walk from a creatively crazy guy in Wallingford, CT — Tom Dooley. Tom suggests...having people line up shoulder to shoulder, facing alternately in opposite directions; i.e., ventral to dorsal. Offer a full roll of 1" masking tape to someone in the file. Ask that person to stick the tape end firmly to his/her body at about waist level (take a round turn), and pass the roll to the next person in line, who sticks the tape to him/herself (no round turn) and passes it on, etc., etc. When the tape is eventually used up (an interesting process in itself), the sticky queue is given a destination that they must try to reach as an encircled group and, of course, without parting the tape, which is akin to — a breach of faith, tearing the group asunder, ripping up shreds of intent or, more seriously, rending the group functionally impotent.

The name, Sticky Wicket, is apt, considering that it has nothing to do with the activity, but sounds like it should. The sticky part obviously refers to the tape. The wicket is fun to say, but remains nebulous enough to make people think devious thoughts without consequence — perfect.

It occurs to me that if you inadvertently or sadistically chose a roll of fiberglass tape for this encircling problem, the group bonding might be a bit more permanent than you bargained for.

**Barnyard**

I always thought of this zooey game as a primary grade activity until I tried it recently with an adult group — they loved it; which puts more bite in the belief that, concerning play and adventure, people are people. Nonetheless, I'm still not advertising this game for middle school or junior high until I hear from someone else that it works.

Here's how. Print the name of an animal (no giraffes) on a 3"x 5" card to number half the group. Then do the same thing again, so that student and card numbers are equal. You will have two dogs, two cats, two cows, etc. Hand out the cards so that everyone knows what animal they are, and then collect the cards. No fair indicating what animal you are.

The simplistic object of this cacophonous activity is to find your genus and species partner with your eyes closed (blindfolds, if necessary, but I don't like them). To be more specific, if you are a cow, MOOOOO; if you are a ...you don't really need to know any more, do you?

When all the animals have found one another, you shout "NOAH'S ARK," and all the pairs crowd into the nearest bathroom two by two and stay there for forty days and forty nights until...

For adult groups, you might want to change the game to *Auditory Chordate Referencing Identification Dichotomy* (A.C.R.I.D.).

43

Don't forget to collect all your animal cards. Failure to do so will result in (1) Having to make another set (2) Possible inter-species pairing (3) An unhappy barnyard.

Excuse my fit of facetiousness — *Barnyard* **is** a halfway decent game.

## Story Lines

Initiative problems are obviously fabricated scenarios that challenge a group to communicate, work together, and come up with a workable solution to the situation. I have found that most people enjoy a bit of fantasy and imaginative role-playing as part of the presentation and the solution.

The following scenarios were made up and sent in by Jo Feldman of Boulder, Colorado. The emphasis of each story line attempts to underline ecological awareness and adds to the enjoyment of the situation. Jo writes, "I developed a new story for each course element which covers a specific environment topic, such as oil spills, deforestation and nuclear accidents. The group leader can point out that the stories are based on real situations and ask the group how they feel about these topics. For example, past discussions have focused on feelings of hopelessness about present day environmental problems, and on what small steps each individual can take to live a more ecologically sound lifestyle."

**Porthole** — Tell the group that there are about 500 to 600 oil tanker accidents per year, ranging from minor oil tank leaks to tanker collisions, which spill approximately 2 million gallons of oil per year into the ocean. With feelings of pity and sorrow, tell your group that the oil tanker just happens to be one of those unlucky ones to have an accident and now they must get through the porthole to the lifeboats below.

**All Aboard** — After the group has paddled safely to shore and started hiking, have them imagine that they have come into a forested area. There is a thick forest of trees to the right and to the left (of platform), but on the slope directly in front of them, the land has been clear-cut (why?). Now, because there is a heavy rainstorm, a massive mudslide is heading down the hill (why?). The entire group must get on the platform to be safe.

**Beam** — At the beam, you can tell the group the mudslide caused a pile-up of logs that they must cross in order to continue their journey.

**Bird Rescue (Nitro)** — Before you get to the rescue site, stop the group and tell them you just heard (through your internal telecommunication system) that the major story in the news is that a tank ruptured on a super tanker and there is a massive oil spill heading towards the shore and killing thousands of birds. The birds are dying because they land unsuspectingly in the oil, it sticks to their feathers making them unable to fly. Ask the group if they want help. Yes!?! As you hike to the rescue site, you come to a gully they can't cross because it is filled with polluted, toxic water. The group needs to cross the gully to get to the birds on the other side. The bucket of water is the special solution that gets the oil off the feathers.

**Safety Shoes (The Trolley)** — At the safety shoe site (field?), inform the group that this place is the source of that polluted, toxic water. It's a landfill. Acres and acres of land filled with garbage — food, plastic packaging, cloths, soda cans, paper and toxic materials like pesticides, fertilizers and industrial wastes. This landfill has been over-filled, causing the wastes to overflow and drain into nearby gullies and water sources. Have the group use the safety shoes to cross the landfill safely.

**Nuclear Reactor (Vertical Pole and Tire)** — Take the group on a tour of the nuclear reactor plant. Point out that the pole is the reactor core. If the tire is off, the group finds itself caught in the middle of a nuclear meltdown. Without the tire on to cap the nuclear reaction, the core will heat up to incredibly hot temperatures and melt right through its containment tank, causing a major nuclear disaster that would kill thousands of nearby residents, plants and animals. If the tire is on, then the group can decide to dismantle the nuclear reactor due to potential dangers.

**Wall** — Even though the group was successful at capping and dismantling the nuclear reactor, some low-level radiation has escaped. To be safe and end the group's long journey, they must get over the protective wall where they can tell the world what has happened to them."

## Rope Script

Mark Murray (PA employee) returned recently from Denver, having facilitated a workshop there for a therapeutic hospital group. As we shared workshop war stories, Mark also shared a new activity. "At one point just before a meal, I had a few minutes left after doing a blindfold (eyes closed) initiative problem, so I asked the group to keep their blindfolds and to attempt the following spur-of-the-moment initiative inspiration." Each person in the group (seven, I think) was to choose a letter, so that there were no more than two of the same letter. Blindfolded, the participants attempted to spell out a seven-letter word using the rope.

Kind of a neat minimum-prop problem when you consider its spontaneous origin, and the extent of discussion and hands-on manipulation required of the participants. Mark therefore gets the spontaneous rumination award for this quarter: 16 oz. of pure cud for future ruminations.

## Quickie Initiative — Roller Ball

*Objective:*

To move an inflated beach ball across a 30' area, without letting the ball touch the ground.

***Props:***

1. An inflated 16-20" beach ball

2. A length of retired climbing rope (or the like) that
measures about 75'

***Rules:***

1. The ball cannot be thrown, kicked, or hit with any part of
the body.

2. The ball cannot touch the ground.

3. The rope may touch the ground.

4. You may have as many people on each side of the 30' area
as you like.

### Solution

Double the rope so that it stretches across the area to be crossed, and is so
situated that the rope sections are parallel to and about 6" apart from one
another (like a set of train tracks). Provide tension at both ends. Elevate the
starting end and roll the ball down the parallel tracks.

After the group has accomplished the roll goal, ask them if they can think
of another way to get the inflated ball across. Hint: Try slingshotting or
fungo hitting with the rope. The rest is up to you; i.e., the group.

### Buddy Ropes

Ever had a hard time getting a group of junior high aged students to hold
hands for a game or initiative problem? Maybe not. After all, developing a
sense of unselfconscious touch is one of the "group" goals that we work
toward in an adventure curriculum approach, but try *Buddy Ropes* if the
squeals, yucks and sweaty palms are too hard to handle on Monday
morning.

Cut a series of rope lengths that measure about 5' long, and tie an overhand
knot in each end. Give each student one length just before the chosen
activity begins. If supplied the ropes (whips) too soon, your compassionate
charges will use them for everything that your instinct says not to use them
for.

Remember the old initiative problem called *Knots*, aka *Tangle* or *Hands*?
Can't remember? Look on page 117 of *Silver Bullets*. Haven't got a copy
handy? That's the one where you ask 8-10 people to stand in a cluster face to
face, and each person reaches across the small circle and grabs someone's

46

hand (like shaking hands), and again reaches across the circle and grabs someone else's hand. If your group is mature enough to hold hands for a few minutes, a grand tangle of hands and arms will result. Then the initiative objective is to untangle the group without letting go of the various grips. Remember now? Not a bad activity, but one that is functionally limited to 10-12 participants..

Now, try Tangle using the ropes. Rather than grasping a hand, grasp the end of a rope. Each person is assigned one rope and is genetically allotted two digital graspers, so when all the grasping is done, this hand-in-hand scenario should come out even. Notice how the tangled ropes allow a better view of what needs to be accomplished. When you begin this problem ordinarily (hands only), the initial view is usually of someone's armpit or the back of their head. I think you will also appreciate the fact that use of the ropes allow more people to be involved. Fifteen participants sharing tangled ropes is no problem. Fifteen tangled people holding hands might result in separated shoulders.

Tangle is just one example of how Buddy Ropes can be used. Think about other games or initiative problems that involve two people operating as a connected pair. The Clock? (*Silver Bullets*, pg. 116). I tried The Clock using Buddy Ropes last week with enthusiastic participant feedback. The centrifugal feeling that develops as the result of trying to beat the clock, is more in evidence.

Ask a line of "roped" (Buddy Ropes hand-in-hand) participants to tie an overhand knot, thinking of the line of people as a single rope length. When finished, the knot will appear in one of the centrally held ropes. Considering the shortness of the ropes, substitute one longer rope (8 ft.) in the center of the line of people. The knot your group is attempting to tie will be easier to establish in this longer rope.

Yurt Circle? Pairs Frantic? Paul's Balls? Off the Wall? Moonball? Circle the Circle? Sherpa Walk? If you have particular luck with one of these, or with any other activity that involves Buddy Ropes, let me know and I'll pass on the curriculum largesse (or caveats, if that's the case).

*P.S. I used 5' sections of retired kernmantle ropes, but I think whatever you have on hand will do.*

### Listening Skills

Did you ever have a teacher pull one of those tricky (sneaky) listening skills problems on you, when you thought you were filling out a serious questionnaire? Of that genre that requires you to read all the information before writing anything, then finding out that the last bit of information (#27 of 27 pieces of extraneous info) informs you that you don't have to do anything? Like I said, sneaky. Here's a better exercise that measures how well you listen **and** follow instructions. The results are visual and unequivocal.

Follow these steps (seriously, I'm not being sneaky).

1.   Make sure each person has a sheet of plain paper (notebook paper with no lines, typing paper) and a pencil or pen.

2.   Indicate that each person is responsible for their own work. No one knows what's right or wrong, so why copy?

3.   Tell students that they need to listen carefully and do exactly as instructed and that **no instructions will be repeated.**

4.   Give the following instructions verbally:

   a.   Place the sheet in front of you as if you were writing a letter.

   b.   Draw a line across the top of the paper, parallel to the top and about one inch from the top.

   c.   Draw a second line across the top of the page parallel to the first line and about 1/2" below the first line.

   d.   Now, draw a third line the length of the page, parallel to the left side of the page and about 2 inches from the left side.

   e.   Draw a fourth line parallel to the third line and about 1 inch to the right of the third line.

   f.   In the small upper left-hand space that you have created, write the word BOSTON (or whatever the capital of your state is).

   g.   In the large, upper right-hand space, write the word MASSACHUSETTS (or whatever state you reside in).

   h.   In the 1" x 1/2" rectangle, print a small (lower case) letter d, upside-down and backwards.

5.   Display the correct diagram that should have resulted from your instructions. Discuss the various line representations and problems that result from not listening carefully.

You will find that in any given group, only 10-15% of the papers will be correct.

This reduced diagram shows the proper orientation of the lines on the paper, as per the above instructions. I chose Hawaii as a state because it's warm there and isn't here.

HONOLULU    HAWAII

P

1/4 SCALE

## Junk Yard Traverse

This is an initiative problem that I have used successfully, when it fit the occasion, but I have never thought of it as a "regular" because I had the mindset that mucho junk was necessary to make the magic happen. Then I received a letter from a subscriber outlining almost identically what I had been doing with groups near various sanitary (and not-so-sanitary) disposal sites. And once again I have in hand that part of the correspondence with the activity outlined, but no name to give credit to. I'll quote the activity (called by the anonymous author, *Here to There*) directly from the letter, and I'll insert parenthetical comments. It's not a bad activity for the right group, in the right place.

*Objective:*

The group must move themselves and their anti-acid resistant junk from one boundary to another while not directly touching the ground — boiling acid pit. (I think just plain acid is good enough. Boiling acid gives off highly noxious fumes and would probably make the crossing impossible.)

*Props:*

Unmounted tires, milk crates, boards, and other anti-acid resistant junk. (Try to include types of junk that can be torn or cut apart so that the participants have the choice of making those kind of truncated decisions.)

The distance negotiated should be significantly longer than the distance of all the acid-resistant junk laid out in a line. This will, of course, necessitate the passing of junk from the end of the line to the new beginning. (We're talking decent distance here — at least 50 yards, I'd say. If you don't think they can stretch the materials in hand that far, give them some more junk. Everyone should be able to choose, from the tons of available trash, a personal bit of acid-resistant stepping-junk.)

This is a good team-builder event and one that can be used to effectively determine where a group stands in terms of cohesiveness. (And, perhaps even more significantly, provide a hands-on opportunity to assist in the confusing decision-making process of determining occupational direction.)

Whoever you are, thanks for reaffirming that fun is where you find it, and that it doesn't take a big budget to make things work.

## 3-D Mine Field

I've been presenting a communication-trust exercise called, "The Mine Field," for a number of years. I thought it was an OK activity for the right group, but it wasn't by any means a workshop standby or a personal favorite. From time to time, I'll ask a workshop group, "During the last few days, which game or initiative problem was the most fun or potentially most useful of all the activities (40-60) that you have tried?" Somewhat surprisingly, the answer has often been, "The Mine Field." People seem to like the unique combination of trust, communication, empowerment, and risk-taking that characterizes the activity.

When I first started presenting The Mine Field, I used only tennis balls as props, set in a random pattern within an outlined area on the ground. On one occasion, as the result of not having tennis balls available during a workshop presentation, I asked the participants to help me spread the contents of my traveling *Bag of Tricks* onto the area outlined by a rope. (I don't use exact dimensions for The Mine Field, but the rectangular area is about 8' wide by 30' long.) The participants liked the idea of creating their own obstacle and particularly enjoyed spreading fleece balls, rubber chickens, rubber rings, beach balls, etc., onto a "blank canvas" patch of gym floor. Obviously, each time the obstacle path is set up, a new mine field pattern is established.

Here are a few rules to help you get started on your own mine field.

1.  Use more or less obstacles to increase or decrease the difficulty of getting to the end of the mine field.

2.  Operate in pairs. One participant is blindfolded (eyes closed) and is located within the mine field enclosure. The second member of the pair is sighted, and must stay outside the obstacle enclosure. Only verbal clues are allowed; the sighted player cannot touch the blind player.

    Allow all the blindfolded players to enter the obstacle course simultaneously to increase the difficulty of careful movement and of being heard.

3.  If the blind player touches any obstacle, s/he must return to the beginning and try again, or simply count the touches for later comparison.

4.  After a successful traverse or at the end of a time period, ask the players to switch roles.

5.  As a variation, ask two blindfolded players to attempt a hand-in-hand traverse. Other variations include: see how few steps can be taken; see how fast the traverse can be made.

Recently, I tried suspending various lightweight obstacles within the confines of the outlined mine field area in order to increase the difficulty of the traverse and also to reduce the predictability of the task. Examples of this "drop art form" included a rubber chicken, a fuzzy length of cows-tailed rope, a horizontally hung 24" length of pipe insulation, a crazy dunce hat, a tennis ball, a shrunken head, a plastic spider, etc.

Use four lengths of 10' x 4 x 4 boards, vertically well-tamped in post holes, to act as the corner supports for overhead lengths of #4 nylon cord. Connect the cord around the periphery near the top of the boards and also continue the cord from corner to corner, crossing in the middle. This overhead set-up will allow you to suspend your playful obstacles practically anywhere over the mine field. Be sure to vary the hanging distance of each item, using *The Goldilock's Rule*; i.e., some high, some low, and some in between — just right.

## Is This The One?

File this under frustration, as it belongs with the *Hands Down, I've Got the Beat,* genre. Ken Demas (PA Trainer) showed me this tricky bit of micro-gridography in a recent workshop. Not only showed me, but had to show me how — I was stumped. Knowing how well most people handle frustration, I couldn't wait to show you.

Reproduce the following grid, making each square about 2" on a side. Fill the square with numbers, as indicated.

### *Procedure:*

With a pointer (pen or pencil), point to the various numbered squares, asking each time, "Is this the one?" The audience is supposed to guess which square the leader picked as the chosen one before the pointing sequence started. To insure honesty, write the chosen number on a folded sheet before beginning. As people begin to catch onto the "trick," ask them to keep the answer to themselves and let the rest of the folks try to work it out as the demonstration continues.

Depending upon your presentation, the gimmick can be extremely difficult to spot. A subtle pointing movement involving fractions of an inch makes the difference.

Here's the trick. Picture each of the 9 squares as being a miniature of the entire grid, as per the first illustration. Whatever position (small number) you point to first indicates the answer. For example, look at illustration #2. If I initially point with my pencil tip at the position indicated by the star, then using the 1-9 grid system as in illustration #1, the answer will be #9 because the * is located in the #9 position. After the initial indicator, I can point to any number I like (because the answer has already been indicated), until I finally point to #9; and the answer is YES. Try this one (illustration #3). If my initial pointing position is where the star is located, what's the answer? The answer is #6. No? Return to GO, reset your "...where's the key?" receptors, and try again.

## Chapter Three
# *Ropes Course Construction & Implementation*

### Double Swing Aboard

Considering the popularity of the initiative problem called Prouty's Landing (Swing Aboard), it should come as no surprise that two of them (two swings, two platforms) in sequence are twice the challenge and twice the fun.

Start either from an elevated take-off area (stump) or from behind a "trip wire." Swing to a 3m. x 3m. portable platform or a large stump. From there, have another vertical rope available to complete an additional swing to a final platform. The idea is to see how many people you can swing onto the two stumps or platforms or combination of the two. Not a bad way to involve an entire group in an engrossing problem. Look for — joy of movement, gregarious glee, unselfconscious touch, sense of team, and "world record" satisfaction.

### The Spider Web — An Illustration

The Spider Web initiative problem is being used more and more by experiential education teachers, because of the predictably good response from participant groups and the equally positive programmatic results.

If you have heard of *The Spider Web,* but thought that fabricating a web was beyond your ability, take a look at the following simplistic illustration that hopefully will convince you to get out there and think arachnidly. Of the dozens of spider webs that I have constructed, I suspect that the asymmetrical web configuration has been different for each one, so don't slavishly try to reproduce the strand pattern that you see here. Do try to make the web openings a reasonable size, and numbering from 15-20.

Note that the prusik knots used to connect the web strands to the peripheral 1/8" cable allow size adjustment of the web openings.

The framing of this useful initiative situation can be pursued in the book *Silver Bullets,* pg. 114 — available from Project Adventure, Inc., Box 100, Hamilton, MA 01936.

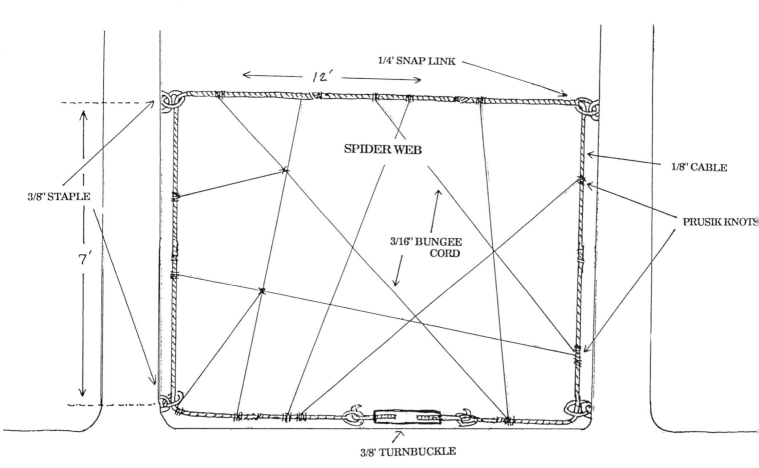

**The Vertical Trapeze**

If you don't orient carabiners and rapid links in the gate-down position, some of them will unscrew themselves over time due to gravity and jostling around; that's a ropes course truism which unfortunately has been proven over and over. Sometimes, due to the above-mentioned bouncing around, the rapid link orients itself into the gate-up position and unscrews itself without your help. To prevent this, tighten the gates with a wrench — now wait a minute — not THAT much; you might want to take this connector off someday. In fact, if you plan to leave the rapid link out there for the entire season or maybe even a year or so, you better put some grease on the threads; otherwise a hack saw replaces the wrench.

I hadn't planned for this to be a lesson in ropes course maintenance, but it's good stuff to know. The reason I mentioned the unscrewed rapid link in the first place, was because of something that happen recently on the

Project Adventure Pamper Pole trapeze. Because of a loosened rapid link, one half of the trapeze fell off the suspension cable. This happened while a participant was standing on top of the pole. (The belay cable and trapeze had just been jostled by another person jumping from the adjacent Pamper Plank for a trapeze that is connected to the same cable.) If you didn't understand that last parenthetical reference, don't bother re-reading it, just picture someone standing on top of the Pamper Pole, struggling desperately for balance and sputtering that half his target had disengaged. The vertically dangling trapeze apparently did not present an attractive challenge to that not-so-stable person, so he decided to climb down. But it looked challenging to me, so I tied in (good ole bowline around the waist — keeps you honest) and had a dive at this weirdly vertical section of PVC rod. I caught it fairly, did a couple pull-ups, was lowered down, and decided to replace what was there (definitely untidy) with a *store-bought* vertical trapeze. We already had another typical horizontal trapeze for the Pamper Plank dive, so this new vertical challenge was well received.

The vertical trapeze has been used now by at least ten workshop groups. From my observations, about 90% grab the bar firmly, and of those, perhaps one in six will hold on. I'm not sure if it's because they grab, then relax, or maybe just a relationship of body weight to arm strength, but the results are predictable — rapid descent and a strong desire to try it again.

To build this unique vertical target, take a 3-foot section of inch and a quarter diameter PVC rod or any kind of similar diameter hardwood dowel, and drill a 3/8" hole one inch in from the end. Then either swage a section of 1/4" cable or splice a length of 1/2" multiline rope through that hole. The length of the cable or rope would be such to hang the trapeze at about chest level to the jumper. Rough up the bar with a rasp to provide the best grip. A smooth section of PVC rod is a bad joke. You might even want to provide a rosin bag for the jumpers, as sweaty palms are a common by-product of this event.

This is a good variation to the normal trapeze jump (you gotta be kidding; none of this stuff is normal). A tip from an experienced jumper and observer — when you go for it, grab high on the bar, squeeze like the devil, and *keep your arms bent*. If you grab at the bottom of the bar with straight arms, the immediate drop is impressive.

### The Hourglass

I seem to remember this high/low ropes course event from years ago, the late 60's perhaps, but for some reason you don't see many on contemporary ropes courses. The Hourglass traverse is considerably more challenging than the Heebie-Jeebie and it's easier to build. Here's how, just in case you might want to build one this weekend.

If your plans include using this event as a high element, install an overhead belay cable (hold on a sec; if you're not planning to build an

Hourglass, just skip right on to the next titled essay — it's in **BOLD** letters). There's a couple mild attempts at humor interspersed among the nuts and bolts of this written pictorial, but not enough to read just for the heck of it.), and high enough overhead so that a participant cannot reach the cable. Approximately 10 feet below the belay cable, drive in a 1/2" staple, so that the staple is oriented almost vertical to the trunk or pole and pointing at the other support tree or pole. Similarly, drive another staple about 4-1/2 feet above the first staple. Repeat the driving of these two staples at the same level in the adjacent support tree or pole, for a total of four placed staples. Pound the staples in so that approximately 1 inch remains between the tree trunk and the end of the staple. If you are attempting to slam the staples into some really hard wood (live oak, eucalyptus, hickory, etc.), you may have to pre-drill the tree to prevent flattening of the curved staple end. If you want to use 5/8" SLES bolts in place of the staples, that's OK. You *have to* pre-drill if using SLES's in hardwood.

Now, measure a length of 5/8" diameter multiline that will extend diagonally from the top staple in one tree to the bottom staple in the adjacent tree, and add six feet. Cut two sections of rope to that length with your Rambo — First Blood: Part 11 knife that you have been wondering what to do with, and put a thimbled eye splice into one end of each rope. Clip that thimbled end into one of the high staples using a locking crab or rapid link. Reeve the other rope end through the bottom staple on the adjacent tree and bring the working end of the rope back to perform a prusik knot onto the standing part, or tie a taut line hitch instead if that's the one you learned in the scouts. Do the same thing between the other two staples (high and low) with the other section of rope.

See how simple that was; certainly simpler to do than read about. What you have essentially done is crossed two fairly taut, semi-slack ropes between two trees. If you don't like the name Hourglass, call it the Two Crossed Ropes Between Two Trees, or more brilliantly, Element #7.

This event *works* (creates the essential challenge that allows the student to achieve beyond their personal expectation and further establishes that necessary link between fabrication and reality — if you know what I mean). Try the high or low variation, or better yet build two — a low Hourglass to establish some skill and confidence and a real high one to allow the practiced student that opportunity to experience fear while performing with pizazz. Please remember to carefully spot attempts on the low Hourglass, and...and, oh yeah...belay the high attempts.


### *Caveat*

Just like on the Heebie-Jeebie, students can tangle themselves and their belay line between the crossed ropes. Extreme cases might result in a rescue scenario. Do you have a long ladder? Can you direct or personally perform a high ropes course rescue? Is the number of the fire department close at hand? Am I being facetious? Think about it.

**Dangle Duo Becomes The Dangle Trio**

In early March, John Lazarus, Adrian Kissler, and I were finishing up some tree work on the new Project Adventure ropes course at the Lyman-Gilmore School in Grass Valley, California. (For you Eastcoasters, Grass Valley is just up the road from Auburn and only a few miles from Nevada City — you know, about halfway between San Francisco and Reno. Look it up.) It's a fine course built between and amongst an impressive stand of Ponderosa Pines.

While planning construction of the Dangle Duo event, we decided to use 10' – 4"x 4" boards for the rungs rather than the traditional 8' long landscaping timbers. The 10' length allowed more maneuvering room for the two thrashing participants and also provided room for an extra climber if you wanted to try a Dangle Trio. (Three climbers — three belays) *Make sure you install two separate belay cables.* Use a router to take off the sharp edges of the boards. Buy clear (no large knots) lumber to preclude possible breaking at the weakened knot areas. All in all, a very functional and visual ropes course event.

Here's a silhouette photo of the event. The person on the event is not a participant (note lack of belay) and is there just for scale comparison. The distance between the first and second rung is 2'6", and each space beyond measures 2" more until a four-foot gap is reached; the regular spacing then increases to 3". If you make the space between the first two horizontal boards doable (dare I say "easy"?), a hesitant climber might be tempted to "just give it a try" rather than "trying it another day." An interesting event to build, climb, and observe. There are 12 rungs on this particular Dangle Trio.

I found out something during the week that we were working at Grass Valley. If it rains hard enough, long enough, water will find its way to your crotch — Gortex micro-pore technology notwithstanding. I also found that a yellow Gorton's of Gloucester lobsterman's hat is the BEST cranial rain protection I have ever had on my balding pate. Absolutely waterproof, warm, and secure. A sartorial tip, however: don't wear your yellow sombrero in downtown Grass Valley. The locals are obviously wondering what advertisement they have seen you in, and if you have any fresh scrod today.

## A Haul Line Strategy

Many ropes course practitioners are using nylon haul cords (lazy lines) to set up their belay ropes (see High Belay Set-Up Solution on pg. 268 in *The Bottomless Bag*). I have heard from a number of people (and have experienced the situation myself) that if not used for a period of time, the nylon haul cord will become inextricably stuck to the top of the S/S belay pulley sheave (in the groove of the pulley wheel). At first, I thought that the cord had become jammed between the sheave and the cheek of the S/S pulley, but on checking two or three of these shear-reduction belay devices, I found that the cord could not fit into a space that wasn't there. After I lifted the cord from the surface of the sheave (having climbed the support tree and pulleyed my way out on the cable), the nylon cord slid smoothly for the remainder of the day.

I finally determined that the sticking was caused by small amounts of sap from the leaves and branches collecting on that portion of the cord that lay on top of the pulley sheave. (This theory was solidified by noticing that no reports of stuck cords were being received from owners of telephone pole courses in treeless areas.) As soon as you broke the adhesion between cord and sheave, the cord ran freely, but strong pulling from below accomplished nothing, except occasionally pulling out the melted-in eye screw or disengaging the Killick hitch tied in the end of the belay rope.

So what can you do to prevent sticking? Try pulling the center portion (say ten feet) of the haul cord over a candle so that a coating of wax is transferred to the cord. Someone said they had good luck using Chapstick, but that seems a bit expensive for treating a number of cords; unless you can talk the Chapstick company into sponsoring your ropes course.

If this technique works for you, or if you come up with a more unique solution (perhaps a touch of slug slime), let me know and I'll pass (slide) it along.

## Heebie — As In Half a Heebie-Jeebie

While working on a low ropes course recently (Mayhew Island, Newfound Lake, NH), we were trying to think of a low connector; i.e., something to act as a challenge that connected two trees in a low element sequence and something that didn't duplicate some other activity or movement on the course. Someone suggested a low Heebie-Jeebie, and that seemed to make sense, so we began the installation. After stringing the taut foot cable and connecting one of the oblique hand ropes, a flash of anti-tedium suggested that I stop there and not install the other diagonal hand rope. What a deal — half the cost for double the challenge: or somewhere near that.

I tried walking the taut 15' cable from both directions and I think starting with the rope in hand makes the most sense. Here's an illustration of a Heebie, if you can't remember what a Heebie-Jeebie looks like. Credit the name to Alan Cantor and Mark Schiewetz of The MAYHEW Program, Bristol, NH.

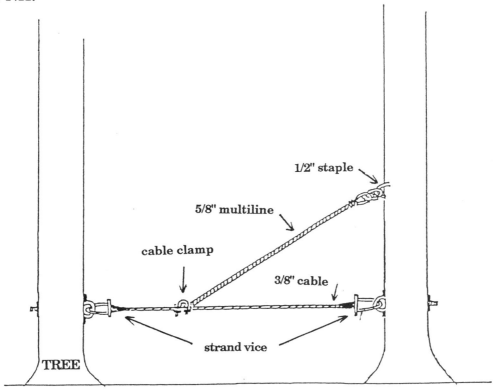

**HEEBIE**

## Wooden Climbing Blocks and Glue

Industrial epoxies (as mentioned in the book *High Profile*; Appendix B, pg. 45), are impressively strong adhesives that can be used in supplementing the use of a lag-shield combination, particularly in the application of wall platform installations. However, recent experiments, both empirical and theoretical, have shown that although epoxy glue exhibits an enormous shear strength, it does not perform well in circumstances exhibiting strong shock loads; a hammer blow, for example. There are not many times when a climbing block would receive that type of blow, unless you were wailing on it with a hammer to test the bond strength, but...well, read on.

I recently took a 2-1/2" x 3" x 5" rectangular mahogany climbing block and "peppered" the back with 1/4" diameter drill holes. I then equally "peppered" a similar sized rectangular area on the wall with a 1/4" hammer drill bit, both to a depth of about 1/2". With Concresive (epoxy) copiously smeared and worked into the peppered center area of both block and wall, I drew a bead of hot glue around the edge of the block and affixed it to the wall so that the drilled and glued areas were directly juxtaposed. (The hot glue was applied **only** to hold the block in position until the epoxy cured.) Twenty-four hours later, I tried to stomp the block off the wall, to no avail. Other members of our staff tried to do the same with identical no-movement results. Then, using a hand sledge, I struck the block until it broke away from the wall — actually the wall broke away from the wall. The bond between block and wall was so strong that a portion of the cinder block sheared off. I have repeated this experiment since then with much the same results, except in one case, the block split. In all cases, the "glue" did not fail, but rather the wood and cinder block split or fractured. I did notice, however, that the glue fingers resulting from the glue pressed into the drill holes did indeed fracture in those areas of the sheared or splintered wood.

The significance of the "failed fingers" may be to try another type of adhesive that has equal holding power and not as much tendency to fracture. Experiments with glued blocks on walls using polyester resin adhesives have shown good results — equal to and generally better than epoxies. (See photo.)

I think either type of adhesive will perform well for wooden climbing block application, with the nod going to polyester resin glue, if you must make a choice. If you feel more comfortable including a lag/shield system, use the glue in conjunction with only one lag per block. This will reduce the measurement step (there's only one hole necessary, which can be drilled anywhere), and only requires drilling one hole in block and wall.

## Gluing Tips

If you have decided to use glue to either supplement the lag/shield system or simply by itself, here are a few practical things to remember:

1. Use a flexible (rubber or plastic) small diameter tube to blow out the residue from the drilled glue holes in both cinder block (brick, concrete) and wood. This is necessary to allow maximum adhesion. Don't use a straw or I'll say "I told you so," as you try to clean an inordinate amount of grit from your eye socket and nasal passages.

2. If you decide to use glue only, leave a non-drilled area about 1/2" wide around the exterior of the block for the application of a hot glue bead. The hot glue is applied only to hold the block on the wall until the epoxy or polyester resin has had time to cure.

3. Remember that each type of glue has a "pot life"; i.e., how long the glue will remain in a putty-like state allowing easy application. Time your work to take advantage of the indicated pot life.

4. Test each block to an extreme (not with a hammer) before allowing student use.

5. When applying the glue to wall or block, use an old credit card (or the like) to work the glue into the drilled holes. Don't just spread the glue on the surfaces and hope that some gets squeezed into the holes.

## The Pardon Me Traverse

I was talking recently with K-Bear (Peter) Quill (a fellow who used to work for Project Adventure and now has his own successful ropes course construction business called Adventure Works), and we were sharing "What's new?" in the wide world of adventure events. You didn't think I came up with all these ideas myself, did you? K-Bear, I'm not even sure this following high ropes course element is the one you had in mind. If it is, thanks for the idea; if it isn't, you're welcome, as always.

One brief caveat: I have not had the chance to try out this high cabled scenario, so I'm writing from a combination of imagination, external stimulation (Mr. Quill), and a plethora of program-related adventure experiences. So, with tools in hand and tongue in cheek, here's the scheme.

After finding two substantial support trees about 30' apart, install two belay cables side by side — both backed up, please — at about 40'. These two cables will look to the world like a set of Tired Two Line cables, except that they are going to be used for belaying rather than shuffling across.

Install a single cable on-center between the same support trees, about 15' below the paired belay cables. You don't have to back up this cable.

Hey hermano; if you comprende what I'm talking at you so far, we are copacetically simpatico. If not, try another, slower run through the last few sentences. Still no go? Are you sure you want to try this thing? Maybe we better get together again a few paragraphs down for the next game or initiative. You're up for the challenge? Eh, muchacho — welcome back!

Drive a 1/2" staple into the support tree about 6" below the paired belay cables. Do this on both sides; i.e., both trees. Measure and cut a length of 5/8" multiline that will extend from one of the above staples to the far support tree. Cut another identical rope length, remembering for both of them to include enough extra (12"-14") to allow an eye splice in one end of each rope. Using a 1/2" rapid link or inexpensive carabiner, clip each eye-spliced rope into one of the respective staples.

Put a ROSA belay package on each belay cable — single-wheel pulley on top with an S/S pulley on the bottom, attached by two 1/2" rapid links. Reeve a section of appropriate length belay rope (double the distance from ground level to the belay cable, plus 8') through the S/S pulley and get ready to DO IT.

The object — you know by this time, right? — is to have two belayed participants attempt to tension traverse across the same cable at the same time, meeting somewhere in the center of the cable for a brief "Excuse me!" encounter. Just think, challenge coupled with cooperation. The possibilities for personal growth are staggering, not to mention the fabulous fear-facilitation factor.

I'll leave you here to mentally experiment a bit. Try: attaching the ropes to the belay cables with a pulley; putting two belayed people on each traverse rope; using the belay ropes as balance support; letting the participants walk to the center of the cable and begin from there, as their pulleys oppose one another.

## Safety Consideration

If the tension traverse is set up as such, use the position of the belayer and the belay rope to prevent either participant from penduluming back into the support tree. Illustration withheld for the same ole reason — I don't draw two gud.

## Mohawk Supporter

In June, I was facilitating a BAT workshop (Basic Adventure Training — I like to call it BAT training, 'cause then I'm the BATMAN), at one of my favorite venues, the Renbrook School in West Hartford, Connecticut. Steve Butler and Nicki Hall (PA trainers of note and accomplished BATpeople themselves), were co-leading the clinic. We had separated the larger group in half and I headed, with my 10 or so people, toward the Mohawk Walk (*Bottomless Bag*, pg. 234). Nicki handed me a 6' pole and I asked, "How come?" Apparently, some of the zig-zagging cables that make up the Mohawk Walk traverse at Renbrook were too long to maneuver across without some ancillary assistance, thus the pole. Considering myself as somewhat of an initiative taskmaster, I pooh-poohed the idea of using anything that smacked of external aid. The satisfaction of completing an initiative problem in the most demanding fashion was the most useful and rewarding approach, right? Wrong. Get with the program, BATman.

Use of the pole for balance and a number of other unique and intriguing functions, left me a pole-fan for future attempts. I particularly liked a limiting rule tacked onto the use of the pole. The pole could be traded from person to person, but could only move forward in relation to its contact with the ground. The pole could never be moved, even an inch, in reverse. Any reverse action and it's bye bye, pole.

Use of a pole as a prop for this initiative problem will be particularly welcomed by those instructors who are just a teensy bit jaded by watching umpteen stumbling students make the same dumb mistakes in the same place seemingly forever. Something new, and it works: better try it.

Substitute a real crutch for the pole — just for fun. You are bound to know someone who has a pair stashed in their attic.

## Staple Placement

Whacking a 1/2" staple into a tree trunk or pole doesn't take great skill, but efficient placement requires experience, above average arm strength and some sense of spatial awareness (mostly of how precariously you can contort your body to achieve a position at height that allows you to deliver a solid sledge blow).

But first, consider the inertial striking implement — a hand sledge. Don't even think about using a claw hammer for driving staples, as there isn't enough head weight; you will end up expending more effort for less results. A one-handed sledge with a head weight of 2-1/2 to 3 lbs. (depending on your arm strength) and a handle length of 12" will do the job nicely. Klein Company makes a dandy sledge with a wide-striking head and fiberglass handle. Project Adventure, Inc., supplies this Moljinar implement: write for current price and availability.

As outlined in a past *BOT's*, staples are placed horizontal to the vertical line of a tree trunk or pole to provide hand and foot climbing aids, or are placed semi-vertically as lead climbing belay anchors. This slightly off-vertical orientation of the belay staple is planned to prevent splitting the wood which may occur if the two staple prongs are aligned vertically to one another. Pre-drilling to about 1-1/2" depth with a 7/16" bit also precludes splitting.

The word *staple* is a noun, defining a U-shaped, double-pronged holding device, but when used as a verb; i.e., to staple..., it becomes a syntactic adventurism referring to the esoteric skill of placing staples in a tree or pole. Here's how to "staple" a tree or pole.

Considering that the staples provide permanent access to high elements (potential attractive nuisance), they should be started a minimum of 10-12 feet off the ground. Using a ladder to obtain that height, place the first staple about 12" above the top of the ladder and to the right center of the trunk. It takes me about 8-10 solid blows to set a staple into oak or maple.There are some woods that require pre-drilling because of their density (live oak, ironwood). Don't try to "macho" a staple into these types of dense wood; you won't win.

Tap the staple a few times to position it, then begin the hard blows. If you notice that the staple is splayed at the ends (not parallel), either grab another staple, or attempt to strike the staple ends together on a hard surface, otherwise the ends will splay further apart as you drive the staple into the wood, perhaps causing the metal to fatigue and fracture.

You will need a tree climber's harness or pole belt in order to work efficiently and safely. So attired, clip in the belt rope around the trunk, lean back, and place the second staple about 18-20" above the first staple and 8" to the left. This will require that you adjust your position to achieve a good striking posture — or use your left hand (non-dominant arm for most people) to knock off some bark and maybe even hit the staple every now and then. Being able to efficiently swing a hand sledge with both hands (and hit the staple) is an attractive job skill: looks good on your resume too.

Move your right foot (arch area) onto the lower staple and your left foot onto the higher one and lean back against the belt in order to use both hands. Leaning back against the belt at a height of 40-50 ft. is a poignant individual trust exercise that takes some getting used to.

Place the third staple 18-20" above the second staple and about 8" to the right. Use both hands to drive the staple if necessary (or if any of your building buddies aren't looking).

Adjusting your belt rope higher on the trunk, stand up on your left leg and place your right foot on the staple you just placed (the third one). Now whack a staple in higher to the left, etc., and continue this left/right pattern to whatever height seems functional for the high ropes course element that you are planning.

Remember to place a vertical staple every 7-8' to act as a lead climb belay point. These vertical staples offer protection points if the teacher has to climb up to replace the nylon haul cord (lazy lines) or to check the belay apparatus, cable clamps, etc. Place these vertical staples on a center line between the left/right ladder-like orientation of the horizontal climbing staples.

As you pass a limb on the climb, it will be necessary to unclip your belt rope and reattach above the limb. Use limbs, limb stumps, natural depressions, and bumps on the trunk to complement the climb and to save staples.

65

If you reach a location on the trunk or pole where you need a two-footed support to work from, place two horizontal 3/8" diameter staples on the same level, and about 10" apart. Since you will be removing these "standing staples," do not drive them as deeply as a permanent staple. After removal, apply a quick shot of 50 year silicone caulking into the open staple holes to prevent bacteria or insect infestation, and to preclude sap flow.

The most comfortable belted standing position is with the feet splayed outward so that the arch of your boots make contact at the tree/staple interface. After standing on staples for most of the day, it becomes obvious why a steel shank boot is such a comfort factor. If you don't have that type of stiff boot, try wearing a pair of bicycle touring shoes — the kind without the cleat works neat.

I have found that carrying a couple staples with grinder sharpened points, to be a significant convenience factor in allowing you to "start" a staple without using the sledge; i.e., with one hand. Holding the staple with the U part cupped in your palm, slam the sharpened points into the trunk to achieve a tenuous placement. This technique is particularly helpful when a strong hitting position is not possible or convenient: you will know when to use it.

**Staple Miscellaneous**

- Use a canvas bag attached to your belt to carry a supply of staples. You will need 20-25 staples to establish a climb and to add protection. If you are stapling a tall tree and need more staples, either carry along a haul rope to resupply yourself from below, or try the following trick. Use a 16 gauge shotgun shell bandoleer to hold up to 25 - 1/2" staples: lots of image (wear it cross-chest) and convenient.

- Sometimes (particularly in pine trees) sap will "bleed" from the area where the staple enters the trunk. To prevent this cosmetic and sticky hassle, try the following: (1) Use the staple points to mark the trunk. (2) Using a caulking gun and clear silicone caulking compound, exude some of this viscous material at each staple mark. (3) Drive in the staple. Predrilling also reduces sap flow.

- 3/8" diameter staples can be used for temporary climbing placement; i.e., when you are setting up the element and need a temporary standing area. Do not use these smaller staples for any belay or permanent climbing situations.

When you want to remove a temporarily placed staple, smack the head of the staple with your sledge from side to side — not up and down. Four or five lateral whacks are usually enough to allow removal by hand.

Remember, if you are placing a temporary staple as a standing aid, only three or four hits are necessary. With a belt on, the angled stance you assume does not put much pressure on the staple. Need I say it — I guess so — Do not put all your weight on a temporary staple.

## *Caveat*

Staples driven into utility poles (particularly when placed in hot, dry geographical areas) must be checked periodically, because of wood shrinkage, to make sure that the pole is not *rejecting* the staple.

## The Endless Zip

I had an opportunity in May to ride the Flying Fox (zip wire) at Merribrook Adventure Lodge in Western Australia. If you remember, I reported on this "world's longest zip" in a previous *BOT"s,* and in that issue congratulated Richard Firth for adhering to the old aphorism, "If it's worth doing, it's worth overdoing." And he certainly did.

Richard picked out a dandy spot for installing the 400 meter (1,350 ft.) zip wire. The cable generally follows the slope of a paddock (Australian for fenced-in area), including the traverse of a gully. Richard reported that it was not necessary to clear a single tree during the installation process.

The harnessed rider climbs a short attached stepladder to a 6 foot high platform and is then clipped in from behind, orienting the participant into the face-down Superman riding position. I assumed that this Peter Pan flight attitude would be uncomfortable for the 40-45 second duration of the ride, but the harness they used precluded any discomfort.

It's a simple clip-in-and-GO scenario, but you have to wait for Richard's dog to bark, indicating that the last rider has disengaged from the cable. Makes sense, right? From a quarter mile away, you can't really see what's going on and shouting from that distance doesn't help much either, so you have to wait for the dog to bark, which he does with predictability and obvious gusto. One rider looked incredulously at Richard and asked, "I'm trusting my life to a dog?" Better than a kangaroo, I'd say.

After the rider picks up sufficient speed, s/he can control their body orientation by extending or retracting an arm, much like a sky diver using wind pressure to change body position. The braking system used is the compassionate bungee-brake, developed by Project Adventure (hands across the BIG sea).

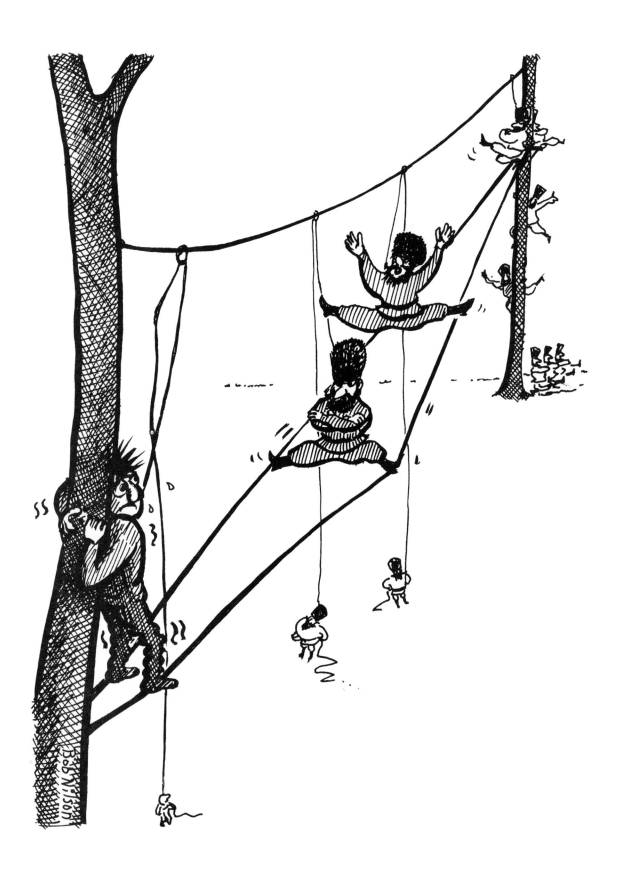

## Chapter Four
# Stunts

### I've REALLY Got The Beat

The only reason I'm telling you about this cacophonous congo-line is because I know it works; however, pulling it off requires a level of Chutzpa that's beyond your basic volleyball skills presentation. Here's the scenario.

Your coed group has been operating together for some time as part of an adventure education class. They know what is expected of them (emphasis on trying), and they have a pretty good idea of what kind of kooky individual you can be. Situation: you need an activity that can involve everyone simultaneously and to each person's chosen level of participation.

Get yourself (yes, you) a drum-like object with which you can establish a simple bass beat; a plastic wastebasket works okay. Establish a basic repetitive beat that doesn't require more than ten hits with your hand; keep it simple. Continue that beat (not fast) as you begin to walk around the room, or wherever you are located. Invite other people to join you in a line, but to opt-in, they must get their own "drum" and attempt to join your established beat. As with any good improvisational section of "music," the beats can vary, as long as the sounds complement the basic beat.

The beat can be copied with almost any two objects that can be hit together, including hands. But try to get the participants to be creative in establishing their own sound; try using spoons, pieces of wood, plastic soda bottles, two bananas, etc. The results of your music-making will vary from din to divine, but considering the range of what's acceptable as music today, there should be something for everyone. The sound and the movement can produce an exciting and memorable experience. I have yet to see a group not respond well to this exercise if the program sequence and timing are right.

Don't feel that you have to continue leading the beat or end it. After you get things started, the beat will flow as to the energy level of the group, and will also usually end itself. Whatever ending manifests itself, be ready to

68

continue functioning with a highly energized group. This is not the time to hunker around the ole campfire and drone, "Kumbaya, my Lord..."

## Hypo-Bubble Rings

I was brought up near the ocean (SCUBA diving since 1964), swam competitively for eight years, and I have never seen anything like this sub-surface display of oral dexterity.

Bubble rings were introduced to me by Erick Rhodes, an adventure workshop participant from Tokyo, who coincidentally swam for the same team (Punahou) in Hawaii that I competed for 35 years ago.

If you are uncomfortable upside-down underwater, this amazing display of well-formed bubble rings offers an oral challenge not to be denied. The trick involves being able to lie on your back at the bottom of a pool at a depth of about 4-5 feet. To maintain this dorsal-down, submerged position, you must either — (1) Let out most of your air, or (2) Drape a set of diving weights over your waist. You must either wear a set of nose clips, or press your nostrils together to prevent water from filling your sinus cavities. (Upside-down, underwater, this filling happens quickly — no fun; don't let it happen. Also, your bubble rings won't look good if you are convulsing and snorting.)

Now, the trick. While staring up through 4-5 feet of water, dimly watching your poolside upside-down friends incredulously observing you, purse your lips and pull them in toward your teeth. Then, with a forceful but controlled burst of air, blow out, maintaining pursed lips. When done correctly (proper lip configuration combined with just the right amount of released air), a perfect bubble ring (looks like a smoke ring) will ascend to the surface. You can expect 3-5 rings if you had to expel air to stay down, and perhaps 8-10 if you use weights.

It takes some practice, but anything this unique and captivating is obviously worth pursuing.

I've blown maybe 50-60 rings so far, and I'm just starting to produce bubble formations that result in comments like, "Say, how do you do that?", rather than, "Karl, what were you trying to do down there?" So, stick with it, and remember, "A good-looking bubble ring justifies itself."

## Cranial Snatch It

I'm sure you have made up a batch of Comet Balls by this time and if you haven't, you should. People love Comet Balls just because they're fun to throw — it's a visual/tactile thing. The reason I'm being so pushy about Comet Balls is that you need a few in order to play *Cranial Snatch It*.

Big commitment coming up — Ask each player to take their knee-high Comet Ball and, opening the end wide, pull it onto their head like a stocking cap. Whaaaat? You have GOT to be kidding, Uncle Karl! No kid in their right mind is going to chance messing up their coif or looking terminally silly for a game. Serious guru-type response: Pick your time appropriately in the program. Use this activity after they have already committed to other bits of zaniness — Dog Shake, Karate Sequence, Fried Eggs, yelling.

Make sure that you are the first one to pull on a Comet Ball. After you get a few nutsy participants to join you, try rotating your head, making the tennis balls spin around — not difficult, but fun. Now you are ready for the game.

Two people jointly spinning their balls (must be spun in opposite directions) approach one another and then try to intertwine their rapidly rotating balls in such a way as to allow an abrupt snatch of the entire knee-high from the other person's head. Winner! Try it again with another person, or just stand there spinning your balls. What a non-skill. What a great non-game.

Couch the rationale for this activity in whatever supportive pedagogic terminology has worked in the past (use words like spontaneous, deinhibiting, self-awareness, etc.), but give it a try. If you pull the knee-high down over your face, you won't have enough sock left to spin the ball, but the other-worldly look makes for a great group photograph.

## Chains

This "game," aptly named CHAINS, was sent in by Murdoch McInnis from Calgary, Alberta. I have never played this game or ever heard of anything like it, and as of this writing, I have yet to experience a sparking chain. I think you will like this: reminds me of some adolescent urban street time I put in a few decades ago. Here's Murdoch's explanation with very few changes.

"I've always called this game *Chains;* here's how it goes. You and your buddy take up opposite positions on a street so that you are about 30-50 meters apart. One of you has a bicycle chain in hand. Now wait there 'till it gets dark and your opponent becomes difficult to see." (Murdoch, you've got to be kidding! Either that, or you have some very patient buddies.)

"Now take the chain and fling it sideways so that it slides along the asphalt (hot top, tarmac, bitumen) making sparks as it travels — real neat to watch. Your opponent has to stop the chain from passing over their goals using their foot — sandals not recommended. If they don't stop the chain, you score.

"Variations on the game are endless with a big enough parking lot; try team action. Be aware that not all chains work (spark) for this game.

Bring various chains and try them out. Out of bounds chains are whatever you want them to be."

"One caution note." (Just one?) "It's a good idea to let folks practice throwing the chain in daylight first." (I can understand that — it gives you something to do while you're waiting for it to get dark.)

Oh Yeah... don't use a chain saw chain!

## Drum Ball

Doctor Rich Maizell, Project Adventure National Trainer and newly appointed (that can't be the right word), Ph.D., told me recently of this whimsical excursion into free-form sound. Rich, you're not kidding, right? You actually played this game, I hope. Well, if not, I like the *sound* of it anyway — so, we'll give it a rhetorical try.

Each person in the group (line up in a circle) has in their grasp something to act as a drum (you know, like a percussion instrument). Now pass around a ball from person to person so that the ball rebounds from drum to drum. You not only get the positive feedback of a good pass, but also the BOOM, PLOCK, WOOMP, or THWOCK of the ball hitting your drum, wastebasket, saltines can, oatmeal container, etc.

After you have determined the tone of your instrument, you and your ensemble can attempt a tune or two, and since it's just about Xmas time, try "You Are My Sunshine..." or perhaps one of my favorites, "Rubber Ducky." Boom for sequence, for tone, for longevity, for...fun.

Thanks, Rich! — I enjoyed writing this, considering that I didn't know what I was writing about.

### Consideration:

Choose your percussion ball with some forethought. A harder ball (e.g., golf ball) would, of course, produce a better, more mellow sound, but the "band" would be well advised to wear helmets. A "Super Ball" would produce good sounds and a dandy workout. A field hockey ball is contraindicated for use in this case, and a shot put is downright antisocial.

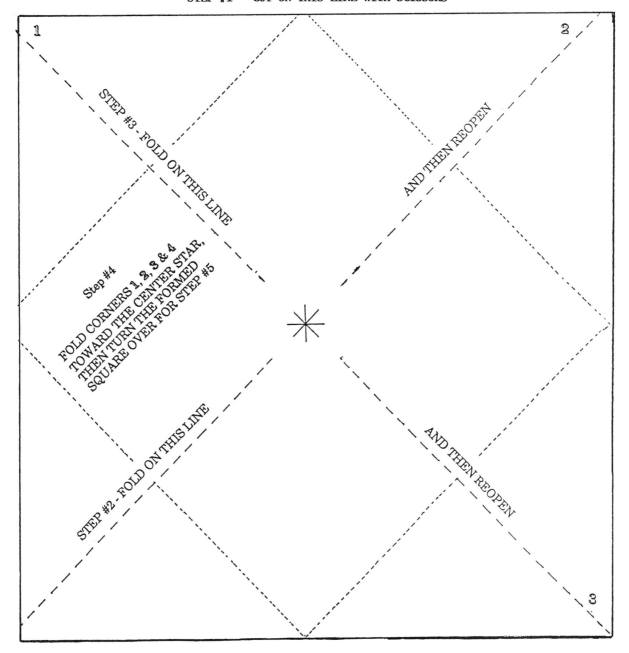

STEP #3 - FOLD ON THIS LINE

AND THEN REOPEN

STEP #1 – CUT ON THIS LINE WITH SCISSORS

STEP #1 – CUT ON THIS LINE WITH SCISSORS

Step #4

FOLD CORNERS **1, 2, 3 & 4**
TOWARD THE CENTER STAR,
THEN TURN THE FORMED
SQUARE OVER FOR STEP #5

STEP #2 - FOLD ON THIS LINE

AND THEN REOPEN

STEP #1 – CUT ON THIS LINE WITH SCISSORS

## Official Cootie Catcher

The above bit of origami is a children's classic and well
worth the couple minutes time it takes to fabricate. Make
one of these for your child (nephew, niece, students) and you
will gain great stature in their eyes. How your friends react
is another matter.

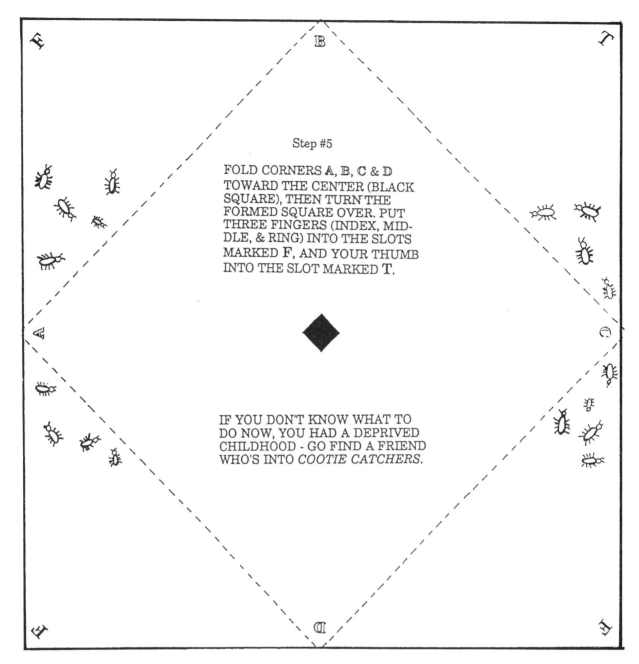

Step #5

FOLD CORNERS A, B, C & D
TOWARD THE CENTER (BLACK
SQUARE), THEN TURN THE
FORMED SQUARE OVER. PUT
THREE FINGERS (INDEX, MID-
DLE, & RING) INTO THE SLOTS
MARKED F, AND YOUR THUMB
INTO THE SLOT MARKED T.

IF YOU DON'T KNOW WHAT TO
DO NOW, YOU HAD A DEPRIVED
CHILDHOOD - GO FIND A FRIEND
WHO'S INTO *COOTIE CATCHERS*.

## Folding and Function Tips

The smooth function of a *Cootie Catcher* depends upon the required folds being well folded, so perform each fold an extra time back and forth.

When you have finished step #5, fold the entire formed square in half one way, and then in half the other way - this makes the fingers and thumb operation smoother.

Once your fingers and thumb are inserted into the proper paper pockets, pinch all four digits together. Move the thumb and ring finger away from the index and middle fingers - this will produce an empty cootie pocket. Then quickly move all your digits back together, and just as swiftly separate them, but this time juxtapose the ring and middle finger together with the thumb and index finger as the other pair. Now you apparently have cooties where cooties weren't - how did she do that?

73

*Chapter Five*
# *Humor*

## Fun Scale

There are measurement scales for everything these days, and if not, the old "1-10" Bo Derek standby seems to suffice. But in the midst of rating everything that can be measured I've never run across a scaling standard for fun, except perhaps those inane, but often useful, 6th grade exclamations like, *Wow! You Beauty! Excellent!! Awesome! Rad!* etc., which words seem to minimally indicate slightly above-normal situations in such a hum-drum way that *right on* verbalizers feel the need to repeat the word or phrase. (That's excellent, man...just excellent!) Anyway, the whole gut-sensation, exclamatory schmear just doesn't provide an exact sense of quality differentiation for people who are serious about their fun.

My suggestion for the time being, and in lieu of anything better, is to borrow the Yosemite Decimal System for future fun rating. The YDS is currently used in this country to rate the difficulty of various rock climbs. For example, a rating of 1 to 5 would designate basic fun situations on a priority basis. A one (1) rated situation would compare to spending a half hour watching Sesame Street. A two or three scenario might compare to viewing a tolerable movie, or perhaps attending a Patriots' game. A four begins to enter that stimulus level where the activity is considered worthy of being repeated. Then the real fun begins with a 5.0; the lowest rating of a genuinely fun time.

Using the 5.0 - 5.10 rating system actually offers a 1-100 scale, but breaks it down into ten categories. A 5.10 effort used to be the highest rating achievable in rock climbing, but as training techniques and gear continued to improve, it became necessary to raise the level of grading standards, and 5.11 became a reality, as did eventually 5.12 and even, beyond belief, a 5.13. (An example of a 5.13 effort would be the successful ascent of an overhanging sand dune!) The climbing experience became so sophisticated that a 1-10 decimal measurement was not enough to differentiate extreme climbing routes, so that beyond a 5.12 level of difficulty, 5.12b and 5.12c categories became necessary and de rigueur. Considering the experimental status of the scale, I'd suggest, for our purposes, ignoring the potential complexity that the secondary letter breakdown entails until the rating situation becomes more user-friendly, and the users establish a more sophisticated sense of fun.

The beauty of a rating scale is that it provides players with a statistically recognized and comfortable comparison that can be utilized toward planning their own fun situations. It's a misconception that people automatically opt for the greatest level of fun available, as it's well known that some player's tolerance for fun at the highest levels is practically non-existent. Check it out! Have you ever been having a great time at an "off the wall" level of participation, and had someone who was obviously not in tune and clearly out of context tell you to "cool it" or "get serious" or "act your age"? That dys*fun*ctional person is not ready for a 7+ level experience, and should either be deferred from the group or playfully avoided.

Unfortunately, it's a fun truism that a 1 to 4 rated participant inevitably brings a group of 5+ players down to their level. The sad consequence of trying to include these people, who routinely rate function over fun (Ed. note — this presupposes that you understand the F.U.N.N. acronym — Functional Understanding's Not Necessary), is a disruption of the fun-flow with an inevitable return to being normal, and who needs that amidst the smiles and action of gaming. Don't get me wrong tho,' normalcy is a function of mundane practicality and is necessary within our get-along-with-everybody-or-else existence. Contrary to what some people strive for (and suffer because of), you can't have fun all the time. Fun levels represent a graphic indication of emotional peaks and valleys; i.e., those psyche situations that occur daily and prevent life from becoming predictable. During peak times, a 5.10+ experience is possible, whereas a 5.3 or 5.4 is about all you can expect on the downside.

What makes all this interesting and less predictable than I've indicated so far, is that the emotional peaks and valleys are in constant flux and can be manipulated by skilled players, IF they understand the mechanics of the fun-flow-flux and are open to its potential for positive change. Another positive that you should consider is that there is no negative to pure fun. To be continued...

## Condoms For Cash

My two younger sons have been seriously collecting comic books for at least five years. Both have collections that are worth hundreds, and depending upon the dynamics of supply and demand, perhaps thousands of dollars. First edition issues rest practically unread in glassine envelopes, waiting for someone or a trend to announce its financial collectibility.

I mention this, because I used to collect comic books also, but I collected them to read and trade with my buddies, and the year was 1947. I paid $.10 for whatever issue I wanted, my boys pay a minimum of $1.00 and upwards of $3.00 for a current issue depending upon the artist, paper quality, issue #, and other comic book esoterica that I don't pretend to understand.

My buddies and I would often get together on a rainy Saturday, and take part in some heavy-duty vicarious hero worship via the colorful exploits of our favorite super beings. I had a cardboard box full of Batman, Supermanboy & girl, Captain America, Captain Marvel (remember Shazam!), Scrooge McDuck, etc.

My Dad was a career military officer, so our family moved often, and during one of those moves, the comics were disposed of. It was no big deal at the time. I had read them many times, and for only $.10 apiece I could restock easily. Then, before you could say Lex Luthor, I was 15 and testosterone was telling me what to do and, not surprisingly, comics were not part of the message.

The boys tell me, dripping slightly greedy tears, that if I still had that grubby box of dime comics I would be rich (whatever that means). Their cost quotes from the most recent comic book catalog of collectibles elicits not tears from me, but gulps of amazement that I at one time stored under my bed what is now worth a not-so-small fortune. So now, marshalling the paradox of perspicacious hindsight, I am going to let you in on the next (50 years from now) make-my-fortune collectible item. One word: CONDOMS.

Stop snickering and try to imagine fifty years down the pike. Will *AIDS* still be the devastating health tragedy that it is today? Odds are that a vaccine will have been developed long before the year 2040. Will birth control depend upon mechanical devices such as shields, IUD's, or condoms? Most certainly, safe and convenient chemical contraception will be regularly practiced within the next ten years.

So what's one of the greatest collectibles of this era? One word. *Condoms.* Get 'em while they're hot. Everyone talks about them in reference to safe sex. They are given away in schools. Drug stores display them prominently. But, is anyone saving them? Condoms. Collect 'em while you can. Think — different shapes, sizes, colors, packaging materials, consistency, by products, advertising, expiration dates. There's a whole world of untapped latex collectibles out there for the entrepreneurial collector familiar with anachronistic trends.

If you happen to acquire any that you think would appeal to a collector, let me know; maybe we can trade. How about starting a condom club? We can vote on the Condom Coordinator position.

## Pre-Remedial Composition 101

*The following excerpts are from essays and themes written by college students. Ungabaleegable!*

"On the night of April 14, 1865, Lincoln went to the theatre and got shot in the seat by one of the actors in a moving picture show. The believed assinator was John Wilkes Booth, a suspended insane actor. This ruined Booth's career."

"France was a very serious state. The French Revolution was accomplished before it happened..."

"Queen Eliz. was the virgin queen. As a queen she was a success. When Eliz. exposed herself before her troops they all shouted 'Hurrah.' Then her Navy went out and defeated the Spanish Armadillo."

"Franklin invented electricity by rubbing two cats backwards and declared 'a horse divided against itself cannot stand.' Franklin died in 1790 and is still dead."

"Bach was the most famous composer in the world, and so was Handel. Handel was half German, half Italian, and half English. Beethoven wrote loud music because he was so deaf."

"Christopher Columbus circumcised the world with a 100-foot clipper, later landing the Pilgrims on Plymouth Rock. The winter of 1620 was a hard one for these settlers. Many people died and many babies were born. Captain John Smith was responsible for this."

"The bible is full of interesting caricatures. In the first book of the Bible, Guinesses, Adam and Eve were created from an apple tree. One of their children, Cain, once asked, Am I my brother's son?"

"David was a Hebrew king skilled in playing the liar. He fought with the philatelists, a race of people who lived in biblical times. Solomon, one of David's sons, had 500 wives and 500 porcupines."

"Without the Greeks we wouldn't have history. The Greeks invented three types of columns: corinthian, doric and ironic. They also had myths. A myth is a female moth."

"Socrates was another famous Greek teacher who went around giving people advice. They killed him. Socrates dies from an overdose of wedlock."

"Life in ancient Greece reeked with joy. In the olympic games, greeks ran races, jumped, hurled the biscuits and threw the java. The reward to the victor was a coral wreath."

"In one of Shakespear's famous plays, Hamlet rations out this situation by relieving himself in a long soliloquy. In another, Lady Macbeth tries to convince Macbeth to kill the king by attacking his manhood. Romeo and Juliet are an example of a heroic couplet."

"Writing at the same time as Shakespear was Miguel Cervantes. He wrote 'donkey hote'. The next great author was John Milton. Milton wrote Paradise Lost. Then his wife dies, and he wrote Paradise Regained."

You have to accept the above with a sense of humor and with a declaration of great sympathy for the English professor that had to red pencil the papers. "...defeated the Spanish Armadillo," is that great, or what?

## Common Things People Say That Aren't True

I was talking with Bob Ryan recently and he suggested that I include a number of these "common things people say..." in a future issue of *BOT's.* I tried to think of (fabricate) a rationale that justified utilizing the space in such a prestigious quarterly and determined that there isn't any. If you really need a reason to enjoy these foibles of self-deception, think: sharing, creative thinking, cooperative brainstorming, awareness...You know, the same ole rationale you use to justify any didactic derelictions.

- Tea has more caffeine than coffee.

- In an automobile accident, you are better off not having your seat belt on.

- If you don't keep exercising, all that muscle will turn to fat.

- The fluid in poison ivy blisters will cause the rash to spread or cause someone else to get it.

- You don't have to be strong to rock climb.

- Let's take a five minute break.

- Having children won't slow you down or change your lifestyle.

- I exercise at least four or five times a week.

- I never fall.

- I'll be right back

- The bigger they are, the harder they fall. (True maybe 2% of the time.)

- You're in more danger driving your car than...

- He's in a meeting right now. Can I take a message?

- I'll put it in the mail today.

- "BARK BARK BARK BARK BARK" — He won't bite.

- I don't get seasick.

- We'll add your resume to our file and call you at the first employment opportunity.
- I have a headache.

## A Child's View of Retirement to a Mobile Park

After Christmas break, a teacher asked her young pupils how they spent their holidays. One small boy wrote the following:

"We always spent Christmas with Grandpa and Grandma. They used to live up here in a big brick house, but Grandpa got retarded and they moved to Florida. They live in a place with a lot of retarded people. They live in tin huts. They ride big three-wheel tricycles. They go to a big building they call the wrecked hall. But if it was wrecked, it's fixed now. They play games there and do exercises; but they don't do them very good. There's a swimming pool and they go to it and just stand in the water with their hats on. I guess they don't know how to swim. My Grandma used to bake cookies and stuff, but guess she forgot how. Nobody cooks there, they all go to fast food restaurants. As you come into their park, there is a doll house with a man sitting in it. He watches all day so they can't get out without him seeing them. I guess they don't know who they are. My Grandma says that Grandpa worked hard all his life and earned his retardment. I wish they would move back home."

## Ropes Course Shoes

*Remember, you are reading this under the humor section; beware of massive tongue-in-cheek and rampant irreverance.*

These brushed-buck wire walker shoes are just the thing for both challenge course sheek and developing that fine sense of trust and daring, so inimicable to higher elevation wire walking. (Note the model's understated choice of contrasting jacket and webbing: the mid-section/collar combination is particularly appealing. A subdued sartorial ensemble combined with that little-boy look, Jim Grout presents a paradigm for your modern **Go-For-It** ropes course participant.)

Fashion notwithstanding, the sequenced photos demonstrate better than words can describe the fail-safe aspect of these compassionate and tenaciously designed shoes. Your hesitating student no longer has to worry about maintaining foot contact with the cable, as even a 180 degree reversal of body position has little effect on shoe/cable orientation.

The third and fourth photos indicate that rare ropes course situation that we in the trade refer to as *loss of participant contact*. This photo representation was only included as an acknowledgement that unfortunate situations do occur and to prepare you for the worst. The editors apologize for any upset of the reader's sensibilities, however, in this case, the rope streaks on the mauve portion of Jim's jacket were fortunately only superficial.

These shoes were not made for walking.

## *Humer*

**Humerous** — A large bone of the upper arm, immediately distal to the scapula or proximal to the radius and ulna: depending on where you're coming from. A fairly funny-bone, but not in the same class as ribs, which are prone to tickling.

Let me be so bold (controversial) as to say, "Humor makes the program." Perfunctorily profound at best and not catchy at all, but if you forget to regularly infuse your approach, presentation, and evaluation with some smidgen of humor, don't anticipate enthusiastic student response.

This doesn't mean that you have to memorize applicable jokes, or wear a clown's nose to get a laugh. What you do need to be aware of and work toward blending with your teaching style are the following pedagogic points:

- *Don't take yourself and what you are presenting too seriously.* I'm referring specifically to course content and how you perceive yourself. I don't expect to change your approach or outlook by listing a few do's and don'ts, but...who really cares (or should care) if someone runs out of bounds from time to time or changes the rules to fit the occasion? It's the level of participation that's significant; level meaning the percentage of people willingly playing and the measure of joy attained. (Evaluators take note: How do you measure the median joy percentile?)

  But what about continuity, self-discipline, and adherence to standards, you say? (Rhetorical license to put words in your mouth — sorry.) Games without consistent rules are a travesty, an unlearning of societal standards that borders on recreational anarchy. Don't worry about (it's me talking again) societal sequencing and civic disobedience; there's an intractable guardian of the rules called THE REAL WORLD that regularly and humorlessly hammers the printed rules home. God help you if you pass GO and ask for more than $200.00.

- *Change the rules of whatever you are doing to fit the situation.* Rules in this context are not made to be written down and certainly not to be consistently reinforced. Remember: If the group likes a certain rule and it makes the game fun and challenging to play, keep it. If the group doesn't like a rule, try playing without it. Also, try rule variations from time to time to see how the group responds. People have been brought up and taught to adhere to rules, so be aware that there's bound to be some

81

resistance when you suggest making third base first and running counterclockwise (Aussie rules).

- *Don't use play objects that the players are familiar with.* If you haul out a basketball, football, or baseball, expect a predictable mind (gut) set about what's going to happen next. Some of the performers who are predictably adept at ball sports are going to bubble, "Oh boy, let's shoot some hoops, spiral a few passes, make some contact and..." further embellish their inflated self-image. Some of the less developed children will cringe, and anticipate another embarrassing episode of athletic maladroitness. The rest (median/mode group) will participate.

  Use balloons, beach balls, deck tennis rings, fleece balls, rubber chickens — something different and fun. As Leo Buscaglia suggests, "...be outrageous!"

- *Use different and unique names for the games that you play and the play objects — names that are fun to say.* If the students ask, "What are we going to do today?", and you say Volleyball, that's a pretty good indication of what the class will be doing; i.e., predictable. Then, it's either "Yippee!", "Oh, no!", or "Who cares?" Tell them that for today only you will be introducing and playing *Valloon*, an existential version of the REAL game, in which you substitute a balloon for the volleyball, and remove the net entirely. (The beauty is you can play anywhere.) Teams try to score a point by _____, remembering that the balloon cannot be hit at a downward angle. The balloon (valloon actually) is served by the _____ team after each change of serve. Rotation and number of hits on each side depend upon _____. You fill in the blanks. Put a little water in the balloon (before you blow it up) if it's a windy day, or if you want a little more unpredictable action, or if it's hot and you just want to get wet.

Is this weird? Probably, but it's got to make you smile and shake your head, and even laugh. That's different, that's fun, that's humer (i.e., humor).

### Crotch Potato

I don't know how much adventure you will find in this simple urban survival scenario, but its use has served me well, well for the last few years, and who am I to keep ideas like this from the world? You know what they say — "Happy crotch, happy whole"... but I'm getting ahead of myself.

Do you ever microwave a raw potato as a snack? You should, because cooked potatoes are a healthy food source, and it's a simple way to tide the hungries. Pop a full-size raw potato in the microwave (don't forget to puncture the spud with a fork to prevent a carbohydrate blow-up) and punch in about 5:30 minutes at max. micro.

When the potato is done, wrap it in a piece of foil (don't put foil in the microwave oven, 'cause for some reason the metal foil causes the microwaves to freak out and not cook the spud), and as you leave for work on a frigid winter day (I forgot to tell you, this idea only makes sense during the winter months,... sorry), tuck the hot potato in your jacket pocket. Nestled there, near the kidneys, it will help keep you warm until the car heater begins to function. Then, when you get to work, the potato will have cooled enough to eat. Instead of a coffee break or smoko, take a potato break — much healthier.

You can also tuck that hot sucker right down into the ole crotch area — feels great when you first slide into a cold car. Of course, you will be adjusting the potato's position as to your personal comfort or immediate need. Guys, I wouldn't even be surprised if you couldn't count on a span of birth control from this simple idea, IF you position the potato correctly. Just kidding,... I think.

## Mute Mouth

As I've indicated in past *BOT's*, I don't like using blindfolds for various initiative tasks. In keeping with the *Challenge By Choice* code, I would rather ask the group to simply close their eyes in order to challenge themselves, rather than offering a cloth strip that not only can become a hygienic hassle, but indicates a possible lack of trust, and perhaps, most significantly, is seldom color-coordinated to each person's carefully assembled adventure ensemble.

While talking with staff member Mark Murray about the use of blindfolds, we jokingly said to one another that what's really needed is a "blindfold" for the mouth. "What a great idea," we said, fully appreciating each other's creativity and willingness to share, concurrently ducking each other's attempt to pat the other on the back. Something unique and tangible to be voluntarily used by initiative problem participants to keep them from sharing those irresistible tidbits of information that have been designated as unknowns or not-to-knows in order to make the problem "work." Mark spontaneously called this oral blindfold a "mute mouth." You have to admit, Mute Mouth is a great name — fun to say, and descriptive in a humorous way.

Mute Mouth is commercially available as a product called duct tape. Buy a roll and cut or rip off an 8" length. Apply the tape directly over the closed oral cavity. Tape placement must be well timed (aimed), because application over an open mouth does not provide a guaranteed sound seal. I have not asked anyone with a moustache or beard to submit to this oral taping, so I'd suggest finding a friend — male or female — with obvious peripheral oral hair and ask them to experiment for the sake of educational research and your future well-being.

Speaking (writing) as a well-shaved experimenter, I can attest to the usefulness of duct tape for the expressed purpose of decreasing the potential for communication. Remember to emphasize the fun of duct-taping your mouth shut. Don't present this oral sealing procedure as a consequence or as a cure for anyone's garrulous tendencies.

## *Caveats*

- When removing the tape, remove it slowly — not like your mom used to take off band-aids.

- Don't ask someone with a stuffed-up nose to tape shut her/his mouth. Common sense, you say? ...Hmmmmmmm

- Don't trade pieces of used tape from person to person. Cold germs will stick to the tape. ...Hmmmmmmmm

- Re-emphasize that using the tape is voluntary.

## Have You Ever...Well, I Guess! Peter, Peter. YES! YES! YES!

## Copy Cat

One of the questions included in the *Have You Ever...* collection is, "Have you ever copied a portion of your anatomy on a copying machine?" Well, that's worth a laugh right there, because we all know the jokes surrounding misuse of the office copy machine. Remember the aphorism, "If it's worth doing it's worth overdoing." Read on...

About two years ago, one of Project Adventure's interns was reading through the *Have you ever...* anthology, and came to the copy machine question mentioned above. He laughingly said that he never had done that, and after a few moments of musing about what was obviously an omission in his personal development as an adventure educator, said that he would soon take care of this lack of corporal copy experience. I thought, of course, that he would take a quick shot of his hand or even a full face profile, but nothing he said or I imagined prepared me for what appeared on my office wall the following day. What you see rather poorly represented on this page still hangs life-sized on the wall to the left of my office door. It is, as you can see, a life size representation of this individual's **entire** body, as produced on a Pitney-Bowes copying machine.

I don't know if this is a world's record or not, but I was so impressed by the originally and zaniness of this bizarre attempt at immortality, that I have left it there as a monument to *joie du vivre.* As you observe the combination of fine detail and nebulous shading, you may wonder (as many have), How did he do that?

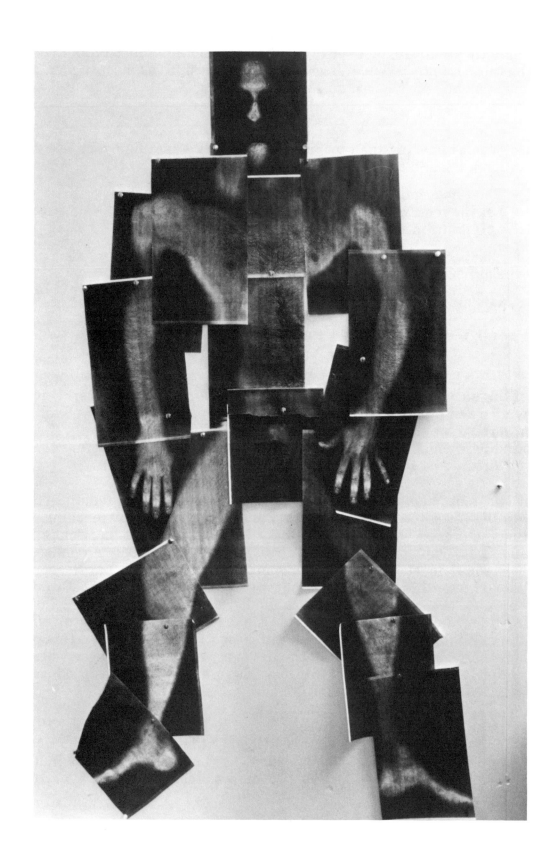

85

## Chapter Six
# *Variations*

## Variations

I've collected these various variations over the past couple years, and rather than slipping them into individual chapters, here's a whole batch. If you aren't into adventure programming, I doubt if this offering will be of much interest, but then if you're not into adventure programming, how come you're reading *Bag of Tricks*? Because you like the author's clear, caring and compassionate writing style? How nice.

## Wordles Redux

It's been a while since Wordles have been included in *BOT's,* so here's a few that I've collected over the months. Answers available immediately after the Wordles, of course, for your instant gratification. I don't mind puzzles, as long as I don't have to puzzle over them too long — say, 30 seconds.


1.   VVIISSIIOONN

2.   CC

      HH

      EE

      EE

      KK

3.   SHAKE USING

4. P 1
   A 2
   I 3
   N 4
   T 5

5. MORE MORE
   MORE MORE
   MORE
   MORE MORE
   MORE MORE

6. RUNNING SCHEDULE

7. RLD

8. BBBBBBBBB

9. SEE P.O.
   P.O.
   P.O.

10. S
    T
    A
    N    CINEMA
    D    CINEMA
    LINE
    N
    G

11. TRUTH TRUTH TRUTH
    TRUTH TRUTH TRUTH
    TRUTH TRUTH TRUTH
    TRUTH TRUTH TRUTH
    TRUTH TRUTH TRUTH
    TRUTH TRUTH TRUTH

12. HE    AD    AC    HE

13. GET    IT

14. SUPERMAN

    LUNCH MEAT

    SUPERMAN

15. THAT

        THAT

        THAT

            THAT

16. L E G A L

17. GNIKOOL

18. RRRRRRR

    RRRRRRR

    RRRRRRR

    RRRRRRR

    RRRRRRR

    RRRRRRR

    RRRRRRR

19. ALLO

20. 2TH DK

21. RE  RE

22. 11

23.  BANGFF

24. SSSSSSSSSS C

25. F FAR E FAR W

## WORDLES ANSWERS

1. double vision

2. cheek to cheek

3. shake before using

4. paint by the numbers

5. there's room for one more

6.  running behind schedule

7.  end of the world

8.  beeline

9.  C - 3PO

10. standing in line in front of the twin cinemas

11. nothing but the truth

12. splitting headache

13. get with it

14. hero sandwich

15. that's right

16. legal separation

17. looking backwards

18. forty niners

19. nothing after all

20. tooth decay

21. repaired

22. one after another

23. starting off with a bang

24. Tennessee

25. few and far between


## Heads and Tails Tag — A Variation

Ken Demas, National PA Trainer, offers this variation of a fairly new game
that he calls "I Declare." The group, well versed in the rules and
refinements of "I Declare," stand ready to play. One person flips a coin into
the air (doesn't matter who, just someone that has a coin), and everyone
declares their heads or tails affiliation by either placing a hand on their
head or on their behind (make sure it's their own behind: this is not a team
game). If the coin comes up heads, heads are IT. All the heads then
charge about trying to tag all the tails. If a tail is tagged, he/she indicates
their tagged condition by putting both hands on their posteriors and
spreading their legs. Uncaught tails can free frozen tails by crawling
through the tagged player's legs and yelling, "TAILS FREE." The game
continues until all the tails are caught, or 3 minutes and 15 seconds have
gone by, at which juncture the coin is flipped again and everyone gets to

redeclare what they want to be when they grow up; i.e., heads or tails. If the coin comes up tails, you can figure out what to do.

I changed things a bit, Ken (can't help it, I'm a compulsive changer), but I think this is basically what you had in mind. Ken, did you ever think of the nomenclature ramifications if your wife played this game? *Claire Declare*. Too much, eh?

## Comet Balls — Again

Try this Comet Ball variation with a just-met group.

Put a 16" x 16" (approx.) cardboard box or a plastic milk crate at each end of a basketball court, setting the container on top of the free throw line.

Don't announce any rules or goals, just take a few Comet Balls and, standing behind one of the boxes, try to loft or lob a ball into the far crate. Toss a few balls on the floor and invite someone (anyone) to have a throw.

This is truly an infectious activity; fun, challenging, and non-threatening.

As more people begin throwing, suggest that a few might want to take a position down-court and return the throws. There's not much chance of getting "beaned" if the throwers are concentrating on the boxes, just make sure that anyone retrieving a short shot keeps their eyes down-court to see what's coming.

I have had to "collect the balls" in order to get people to stop taking one-more-throw. This simple activity is a winner — try it.

## Nutsy

You have just finished playing *Comet Ball Spin and Catch*, and perhaps added a couple minutes of *Cranial Snatch It,* but you don't want to just say, "Put the balls in the box, please." So instead you say, "Everyone bring a comet ball and bunch up over here. Now spin your ball. Good. Everybody spinning? Try to release your ball straight up (don't look up), then put your hands on top of your head (grimacing and grinning at one another) and wait for the balls to come down." OK... time for lunch!

## Comet Balls — Variation

Try this Comet Ball variation with a just-met group.

Put a 16" x 16" (approx.) cardboard box or a plastic milk crate at each end of a basketball court, setting the box on top of the free throw line.

Don't announce any rules or goals, just take a few comet balls and, standing behind one of the boxes, try to loft or lob a ball into the far crate (bounces in don't count, unless you want them to). Place a few balls on the floor and invite someone (one of those people leaning against the wall wondering why they are there) to have-a-throw. Don't worry about being a little pushy to get things started, as this is truly an infectious activity; fun and challenging in a non-threatening way.

As more people get involved in throwing, suggest that a few folks might want to take a position down-court and return the throws. There's not much chance of getting "beaned" if the throwers are concentrating on the boxes, just make sure that anyone retrieving a short shot keeps their eyes down-court to see what's coming.

I have had to "collect the balls" in order to get people to stop taking "just one more throw".

## Comet Ball Fabrication

Slide a used tennis ball down to the tip of a woman's knee-high pantyhose type sock: that's it — that's all.

Supply centrifugal force by spinning the sock and then let go at the appropriate moment. If you don't know when the appropriate moment is (estimation can vary wildly), remove yourself from the vicinity of other people, animals, and automobiles for some practice shots, as vertical and backward throws are not uncommon.

## TP Sprint

Another TP Shuffle Variation (TP is an initialism for Telephone Pole, in case you didn't know).

Place four volunteer "facilitators" on the TP log. During the course of the problem, they are not allowed to leave the log.

Split the remainder of the team in half. Each half moves to either end of the log; i.e., off the log and on the ground. The object is to trade ends as quickly and efficiently as possible, recognizing that the starting and ending positions for each team (same team really) is on the ground at the ends of the log. Place a short length of slash rope perpendicular to each end of the log. That's the start and finish line you are not allowed to step over and into the toxic material — which looks like dirt or grass to most people.

### *Rules and Penalties:*

- The four facilitators cannot leave the log. If they do, each ground touch receives a 30 second penalty.
- This 30-second penalty also holds for all the other participants.
- No props are allowed to be used.

I have seen a group of 18 fairly normal people complete this task in 22 seconds — Go For It. If you aren't *fairly normal*, add or subtract a few seconds as the case may be.

## Categories

Other grouping ploys —

- Considering TP use, are you a scruncher or a folder? (Better know your audience well before you lay this one on them.)
- Who is wearing some kind of jewelry (wrist watches don't count)?
- Shoe size (make it a co-ed grouping).
- Favorite type of restaurant (Mexican, Chinese, Italian, etc.).
- When clapping hands, which hand is on top?
- Draw a circle in the air with your finger. Do you move finger clockwise or counter-clockwise?

## Have You Ever...Circle Game

Starting on page 141 in *The Bottomless Bag* is the beginning of a list of questions (500+) that are prefaced by the question, "Have you ever..." The value of asking and answering these fun-based queries is to be able to find out more about the members of a group in an unselfconscious way. Use of this circle-game format allows even the most self-conscious students to participate and learn more about their peers. It goes like this.

Ask the group to arrange their chairs in a circle so that there is a chair for each participant, except for the volunteer IT person who stands in the center of the circle. The center person then asks a "Have you ever...?" question. If a seated player answers the question YES, then that person must leave his/her chair and try to find an empty one. If they answer NO, that person stays in his/her chair. If the question, "Did you brush your teeth this morning?" is asked, all those who did brush jump up and dash for a vacated chair, while those who forget or just didn't, stay in their chairs.

The person in the center rarely stays for more than one question, because their positioning allows them to grab an empty chair with dispatch. Whoever is left without a chair is responsible for asking the next question. If that center person would rather not (too timid) ask a question, they are free to trade positions with someone (and there's always someone) who apparently has a question they are burning to ask.

## Ambulatory Have You Ever...

There has been some mention around Project Adventure that the sitting circle game **Have you ever...** is doing a job on the chairs at our workshop venue in Ipswich. I'll have to admit that not wanting to get caught in the center of a circle is sufficient reason for throwing your body toward any still vacant chair, but as a result, chair legs are becoming an endangered support mechanism. Here's a way to beat the seat.

Ask your group to line up in a circle and join hands. You stay in the middle of the circle to ask the first question (notice — no chairs). Rules are the same as the seated version; whoever in the hand-held circle answers YES to your "Have you ever..." question must move to another position in the circle (not immediately to their left or right). Those who answer NO stay put with their arms and hands extended. It becomes obvious who the last person is — that panicked player dashing about with arms extended, trying to find a pair of free hands in the rapidly filling circle. As you can see, the game remains the same, but utilizing this propless version, you don't have to scout around for chairs or worry about what's going to happen to them — because it will (happen, I mean).

Try using Buddy Ropes to establish this hand-in-rope circle.

## More Have You Evers

...refer to *BOT's* #30 and 31, or *The Bottomless Bag,* pg. 141.

> ... been in an auto accident in a vehicle that deployed an air bag?
>
> ... had five pieces of Double Bubble (or Bazooka) bubble gum in your mouth at one time?
>
> ... run a STOP sign at more than 30 m.p.h.?
>
> ... dug up a human skeleton?
>
> ... passed out underwater?
>
> ... gone two weeks straight without wearing a pair of socks?
>
> ... drowned an ant purposefully; i.e., string around thorax with pebble anchor, etc.?
>
> ... kept a street sign in your bedroom? (E.g., STOP, YIELD, 30 M.P.H.)
>
> ... seen a "green flash" as the sun sets over the ocean?
>
> ... removed a bottle cap with your teeth?
>
> ... ridden or operated a jet ski?
>
> ... been in a plane while it breaks the sound barrier?
>
> ... flipped a video game?
>
> ... fired an arrow straight up?

... seen **more** than three theater movies in a row? (videos don't count)

... been an extra in a Hollywood movie?

... owned a tuxedo?

... spun a doughnut with a motorcycle?

... let your fingernails grow more than an inch long?

... skated more than two miles in a direct line (without turning around)?

... caught a wave on a surf ski?

... swallowed a live goldfish?

... been accused of having an accent?

... paid extra for a vanity plate?

... killed a crow with a shotgun?

... sung along with one of your favorite groups, recorded the effort, and recognized that you are never going to make the big time?

... worn an oral prosthetic device to keep from grinding your teeth at night?

... sheered a sheep?  ...seen it done on site?

... been buried vertically in the sand up to your neck?

... hung up on a telephone solicitor after having identified yourself?

... cut a golf ball open and had the liquid center explode in your face?

... tossed a caber? ...tossed a caber successfully (i.e., end over end) ...tossed a caber in competition?

... climbed a utility pole over 90 feet high?

... been in bomb shelter?

... successfully climbed a vertical sand dune?

... seen a section of 7/16" goldline rope break?

... been shot by a slug measuring .22 caliber or more?

... tried a pinch of Skol twixt your cheek and gum?

... driven across the continent, paying less than $30.00 for petrol?

... been called to attention by a drill instructor?

... fanned a revolver using live ammunition?

... been stung by: a honey bee, wasp, hornet, yellow jacket, white faced ground hornet, scorpion, black widow spider, brown recluse, tarantula, Australian bull ant, red fire ant, sea anemone, fire coral, sting ray, stinging nettle, green head, black fly, mosquito, cone shell, Portuguese man-o-war, jelly fish.

... wondered WHY?

... spent the night in a hammock?

... painted an entire automobile with a paintbrush?

... chummed for sharks with human blood?

... worn a money belt?

... eaten Kim Chee?

... baked a cake or pie from scratch?

... cooked a dinner for 6 people or more?

... kept a batch of sourdough yeast going for more than two years?

... grown an avocado plant from a seed using toothpicks?

... made whip cream using a hand beater?

... shot whipped cream from an aerosol can into your mouth so hard, whipped cream came out your nose?

... given yourself a haircut?

... been able to cut a long piece of something with a scissor without sympathetically using the muscles of your jaw?

... eaten one peanut when many were available?

... wondered why or how your rear view mirror can be flipped at night and still allow you to see the cars behind you?

... bungee jumped over 100 feet?   ...wanted to?


## Swat Tag Variation (*Silver Bullets*, pg. 45)

After you have introduced the game *Swat Tag* and play (using two "swatters"), has begun to flow, ask everyone in the circle to join hands. Now, when someone is swatted and has to chase the swatter into the center of the circle, his/her absence from the circle's perimeter causes an easily recognizable gap. Introduce the rule that when a gap is formed as above, that gap can be filled by anyone else in the circle who chooses to do so. The person who was swatted now has to search the perimeter and try to spy where the escape gap is located. If two or three changes of position have taken place, this quick visual search can be frustrating. The problem in the past, in trying to allow gap filling, was that no one really knew where the gaps were located as people shifted and jostled with the flow of the game. Holding hands (or not holding a hand) offers a quick and definitive indication of where a gap is located.

Try using *Buddy Ropes* to extend the size of the circular play area.

### *Janepaulfredsueiradavepeggy, or Hustle Handle*

Here's a useful low-key game that won't do a thing for cementing names in anyone's memory, but serves as an ideal icebreaker for very adult and seriously mature groups of potential children.

Arrange everyone in a circle, including yourself, by suggesting, "Line up in a circle." Locate a digital stop watch within the group (someone always has one), and announce this as a timed event. Say your first name with gusto, and start the watch at the same time. The person next to you (choose clockwise or otherwise) follows by saying their first name, and the person next in circle says theirs, etc., etc., *asfastaspossible,* until the whole circle is finished; i.e., back to you — stop the watch.

This spitting out of faintly recognizable sounds turns into a speed-slurring of what used to be a series of distinct names. The useful aspect of what seems to be useless sounds in the round, results from the intensity of working together to achieve a series of improbable speed goals. It is continually amazing to me how much faster a group can collectively say their names in sequence when they start getting competitive with themselves.

As leader and facilitator, start the activity with subdued enthusiasm and as the group continues to lower their time, let your growing excitement (which reflects theirs) grow apace. When the group goes for the ultimate record, be a cheerleader, be a coach, be whatever you need to be to allow an unbridled flow of intense participation.

After the team (the A Team in this case) has had a few chances to establish a decent speed record, allow the B Team to have a go. Tell the A Team that they did very well, but now it's time to get really competitive and allow the B Team to establish their own mark. If you haven't caught on yet, the B Team establishes their identity by spitting out the names in the opposite (clockwise/counterclockwise) direction. This is great fun, because at first they don't know what to make of the situation or your bizarre suggestion.

Become a cheerleader for the B Team now and see what happens to the effort and resulting time.

After both *teams* are satisfied with their attempts, ask the group with which team (A or B) they felt most affiliated. This entire scenario lends itself to a useful discussion of the role of competition within this type of curriculum setting; i.e., competition against self as compared to the more typical and negative win/lose situation.

*Ed. Note: This is not a good game for learning names – nor should it be.*

If you can say the name of this game as typed above without a mistake and no tongue-stumbling, try saying TOY BOAT five times quickly. No, no, no – not *toy-boat-five-times-quickly,* just the two words TOY BOAT. If you can do that, you are officially excused from the next activity that you don't want to be involved in...I'll write a note for you.

## For Peripatetic Spiders Only

Alan Jones, lecturer in Outdoor Education in the U.K., writes of a spider web variation that allows him to carry the "web" with him as he hikes with a group. He ties hula hoops together with short sections of string (I'd use pieces of 3/16" bungee cord), and when the situation presents itself, he undoes the hoops and suspends them from two support trees. The hoop sizes can be varied to make the problem more diverse. Good-O, I'd say.

## Body Bridge It

While working with Telecom Company in Sydney this last April, I started to get the materials together for the initiative problem *Bridge It.* As it turned out, I couldn't find a number of the props that I was looking for. So I thought a thought and *Body Bridge It* came out the creativity slot. This was another example of necessity being a mother and serendipity coming to the rescue. Here's what you do, or don't do if you are already familiar with the initiative problem (*BOT's* #10), or *Bottomless Bag,* page 256.

Rather than offering a plethora of props to build the bridge, suggest that the participants use their bodies for the bridge structure, and then add whatever small props you like to add some variety. By suggesting that they use their bodies as structural support you are also suggesting that they all integrally involve themselves in the solution. Not being a part of the solution was often a problem before, now there's no way out. *Challenge By Choice* is still the approach of choice, but even so, it's hard to go off for a smoke with someone lying on your stomach or grabbing your ankle, or whatever.

Feedback that I have gotten from the participants and Executive Reach facilitators seems to indicate that this corporeal variation not only increases the level of participation but is viewed as more fun; always a plus.

## Passionate Line-Up

Now wait a minute, this isn't what you think (hope) it is. When you have the group in a line-up mode (by age, height, distance they had to travel to the site, blood type, etc.), ask them to line up as to how passionate or passive they think of themselves. Passionate to the left, passive to the right, or somewhere in between. What then? Entirely up to you...I'm into empowerment.

## Fire in the Hole Revisited

When you have an activity that is this blatantly fun and functionally useless, there's bound to be a booming variation, and so there is...

Refer to *Silver Bullets*, pg. 51 for the basic rules (?) to the activity *Fire-in-the-Hole*.

Now, line up in a circle with a charged (filled to the max) balloon between each participant; i.e., occupying the space from ventral to dorsal between igniters. The group can decide to attempt an H-bomb (H=holistic) explosion by everyone pulling on their partner simultaneously (instant gratification), or go for the more sequential series of charges that signals a group who wants to prolong the kinetic psychomotor display; i.e., likes squeezing one another. Either way, F.I.T.H. becomes further entrenched as *the* event for "all seasons and no reasons."

## Teeter Totter

The Hanging Teeter Totter and the more typical land-based fulcrum variety are not the most popular initiative problems; mostly because of the kinetic finale that inevitably results from the group falling off or disengaging themselves from the element. However, if you are enamored of the event and want to reduce the chances for bodies being tossed about, place the long teeter totter balance log on top of and perpendicular to a shorter log of equal diameter that is placed on the ground. Using a chain saw, cut a small notch in the bottom log to keep the top log from skewing left and right. Too simple? Too true! (No diagram offered because the text says it all, and my scribbling smacks of 2nd grade homework.)

## Unholy Alliance Tag Team

The Four-Way Tug-O-War (Unholy Alliance) is a zinger of an event: physically demanding, but engrossing and masochistically fun. However, if this bit of oxygen-debt curriculum is your choice for day 6 lesson planning, better have something else in mind for the latter half of the class: active participation as an Unholy Allier can produce a noticeable reluctance (corporeal shutdown) to do anything afterward that requires an act more physical than breathing.

So, to extend your curriculum time, suggest a tag team set-up. Rather than dividing the entire class into four equal groups, ask the members to arrange themselves into a tag team situation (three groups of two, perhaps), so that only two players at a time are allowed on the pulling rope. This ploy not only allows intermittent rest, but encourages strategizing, gamesmanship (I refuse to change the gender of certain words), and high-speed cooperation.

Students who have watched "professional" wrestling should respond well to a tag-team approach.

### Zip Wire — Trust Fall Start

Some students want to experience a second or third try on the zip wire ropes course element, and why not, it's an exciting ride. If those second riders (or you) want an escalated challenge at the onset, try the trust fall start.

After clipping into the zip pulley rope, stand facing the tree; opposite the direction that you will be zipping. Using the tree platform as a trust fall platform, fall backward with your hands at your sides just as you would during a trust fall sequence. The length of the zip-pulley rope, and the fact that the pulley begins to roll as you lean back, produces a longer, unsupported fall than anticipated. Try to complete the fall (until the zip begins) without reaching up and grabbing the rope.

This extra challenge is **NOT** recommended as a first ride attempt. Also, the trust start **CANNOT** be attempted if the zip cable has been installed to allow a sitting start on the platform.

### Wild Woosey — Using Buddy Ropes

The Wild Woosey is the Wild Woosey, etc. — I never thought I'd see a worthwhile variation, but here's one that adds a tingle of titillation and communicative decision-making. (I know, sometimes the words don't make a lot of sense, in or out of context, but stick with me, I'm just asyntactically enjoying myself.) Provide the two participants with a 4-5' long rope for use as a support prop during the cable crossing. The old trick of attempting to pull against one another (doomed without the use of ropes) now makes sense. Adequate spotting outside the cables is necessary for safety.

The use of the ropes is not meant to take the place of the classic A-frame person-to-person attempt, just a variable to provide that important "something" which allows a student to approach the element in a uniquely challenging manner.

**Electric Fence Variation**

The quintessential love/hate initiative problem.  If you have dismissed this useful and highly portable initiative problem because of the potential for injury, here's a way to slightly change the physical set-up to prevent the tempting and sadly satisfying airborne launch technique.  (See *Silver Bullets*, pg. 136, for the basic rules and framing of this initiative problem.)

Historically, the problem has been that large participants regularly throw small participants over the "electric" rope.  Being launched in such a way has a tendency to produce airborne disorientation  resulting in damage to the flight object's landing gear — broken wrists, ankles, etc.  To prevent people-throwing (at last, the crux), string an identical section of "electrically" charged rope parallel to and two feet above the original electric rope.  The twenty-four inch opening between the top and bottom strand is the exit area — force fields are extant above and below.  With such a small target opening to exit, human projectiles no longer make sense.  Simple, eh?

Use 1/4" bungee cord to act as the "electrical cables."  If someone even barely touches this stretchy cord, it vibrates noticeably — a definite plus for the keeper of the kilowatts.  Also, if someone is deposited accidentally onto the cords, either one or both of the cords will stretch to the ground, preventing rope burns or dangerous fulcrum falls.

**Trolley switch** — As your group attempts to duck-walk their rope-festooned boards across whatever devious A-B traverse your benignly sadistic imagination has concocted, require that whomsoever falls from a board into the putrescence must return to their same position on the boards, but facing in the **opposite** direction.  Lovely, just lovely...(See Trolley, *Silver Bullets* pg. 118.)

**Truncated trolleys** — If you are tired of transporting 16' lengths of 4 x 4 boards in or on your vehicle, try this foreshortened trolley approach.  Cut your 16' lengths in half.  In two ends of each 8' length, pre-drill the center with a 1/2" bit and turn a 5/8" SLES (shoulder lag eye screw) into each hole.  Connect the two eye screws with a 1/2" rapid link.  The centipede-like trolleys that result are a bit more difficult to navigate, but the advantage to segmentation is largely the ease of transportation to and from the initiative site.

**Sticky Steps (A very portable variation of The Trolley)**

There's a useful little hand saw on the market called a Stanley Short Cut.  It's a tool box saw that's about 15 inches long and is advertised to cut 50% faster, because of *aggressive tooth design*, than conventional saws. I'm not sure what a conventional saw is, but I guess it's one that cuts 50% slower than Stanley's.  There's a photo of an open-mouthed, heavily-toothed shark on the packaging sleeve that has nothing to do with the saw, but I guess is there to convince you not to use the saw in a marine environment. I've said all this to indicate you need a saw to cut some sections of 4 x 4, and since I just bought the one above and liked it, I thought you would too...but, any ole saw will do really.

You might want to read to the end of this handy little discourse to find out what I'm leading up to and before you start cutting up your 4 x 4's. But even though I'm out of sequence here, I'll just keep going, if you don't mind.

Measure off 12" sections, and zip through that try square scribe line with your *shark-toothed* short cut saw. (See, I was just kidding about not knowing why the shark's photo was featured.) Collect all those one-foot sections (one section for every participant) and countersink (use a 1-1/2" bit) one third of the blocks to look like illustration #1. Countersink the second third to look like illustration #2, and finally for the third third, to look like illustration #3. With a 5/8" diameter bit, and starting in the center of each countersunk hole, drill all the way through each 4 x 4.

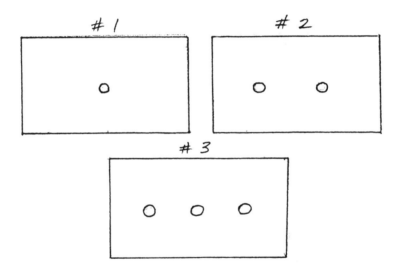

Cosmetic hint — Stop drilling when the point of the bit just breaks through the far side of the 4 x 4. Turn the board over and begin drilling where that pin prick hole is located. Doing this prevents the wood from splintering as the drill bit eats through the final 1/4" of wood. Just a common woodworking trick, but it may impress somebody, and it does produce a neater hole.

Cut some 6' lengths of 1/2" multiline to equal the number of holes drilled, less seven. Back splice one end of each rope and tie an overhand knot in the other end. Place all of these accumulated props in a hodgepodge pile and offer the following challenge...finally the crux.

*Using these assembled props and none others, attempt to move your group from point A to B in the quickest, most efficient manner without touching the ground.* Sound familiar? I'd guess so, but the solution(s) are unique, interesting to both participant and facilitator.

### *Rules, Considerations and Variations:*

- No one may touch the ground (floor) with any part of their body. If ground contact is made, that person must either return to the start or receive a time penalty — depends upon your presentation.
- No one may operate independently, but must maintain physical contact with at least one other person.
- The blocks may not be used as simple "stepping stones."
- You may use as few or as many of the props as desired during the crossing.
- The props do not have to be returned to the start, but may be used for more than one crossing.

As a result of the rules format, you are trying to get the participants to make some decisions as how to best use the props. For example, if you put a rope through the middle hole, then stand on the block with rope in hand, you have essentially fabricated a no-springs pogo stick. Then by initiating a controlled hop, surprisingly easy forward progress can be made, and, to abide by the rules, this hopping must be done in tandem. Example 2 – Insert two ropes, one each, into the two outside holes . Use a block per foot and grab a partner. Or (example 3), have two people stand side-by-side with a single rope block for their inside feet and a double roped block for each outside foot. Variations and decision-making go foot-in-foot.

- Remember to remove the ropes from the blocks before you allow another group to make an attempt.
- Turned ankles are a possibility, so do not allow running attempts.
- Rout the edges of the 4 x 4's before cutting into sections.
- Duffel bag transport with a smile.

If you fashion the board lengths to only 4' long, the event begins to resemble a segmented centipede. These shorter lengths can also be separated for use by special needs groups or be utilized for the competitive urges of fleet-of-foot board stompers.

### Group Juggling Variation

Group Juggling is explained on pg. 112 of the book, *Silver Bullets*.

As the fleece balls are flying around the circle, ask each person to make a sound as they either catch or throw a ball. Group juggling involves considerable sensory stimulation as is, so the addition of multiple sounds creates a grand level of cacophonous chaos. Emphasize choosing or creating unique sounds.

### Name Game Variation

I just tried looking up the game, **Name Tag**, so I could refer to it as previously presented in *BOT's*, or in a Project Adventure publication, but I can't find it. Did I ever write about it? Anyway, rather than flipping through back issues (it's not in *Bottomless Bag*), here are the basic rules — so I can tell you about a variation that Lee Gillis (National Trainer from Georgia College) passed along. It all seems a bit circuitous, but the game and the variation are worthwhile. Steve Butler and I made up the game one night about five years ago in Syracuse.

This is a name-reminder game, so the group would have had to previously played one of the other name games that associates faces and names.

Ask the group to close their eyes and with "bumpers up" (hands protecting faces) to slowly mill around until you say, "Stop." When the group is nicely separated and disoriented, tell them that you are going to tap somebody's shoulder and say aloud that person's name. The tapped person immediately opens her/his eyes and quickly finds someone nearby to tap and name. This procedure continues until everyone has had a turn.

Tell the group before you begin, that their attempt from start to finish will be timed. Try this activity at least twice so that the group gets the opportunity to best their previous time, and hopefully allows forgetful folks (like me) to wet-cement a couple more names in place.

As a convenience to the tapped and often frantically searching player, each person who has had a turn should kneel or sit down to indicate that their tag turn is complete.

It's embarrassingly interesting to watch a tapped player open his/her eyes, look directly at the person in front of them, then dash off to tag someone at a distance. It's painfully obvious why the vis-a-vis person is ignored, but the forgetting and enjoyment of the consequence is shared, as names eventually become people.

**Variations** — When a person taps someone and says their name, they must join hands with that person and move as a pair to tap and name a third person, etc., etc. The game ends (stop the watch) when everyone has joined hands.

There is a certain amount of performance pressure associated with this game. To make it more team-oriented, require that everyone (with open eyes) shout out the name of the person being tagged.

## Another Name Game Variation

In the September '89 issue of *JOHPERD*, page 6, I noticed a variation of Toss-A-Name Game (*Bottomless Bag*, pg. 8) that reads like a good one. After the ball(s) has been tossed around for awhile, and it's obvious to you that the players are becoming comfortable with the various names, incorporate a group shout. As the author of the column (Torbert) writes, "...as the object is thrown to a player, the thrower no longer calls that person's name. Instead, all those in the group who remember the catcher's name, shout it out."

This loud verbal reinforcement of what most people already know is satisfying to the shouters and to the person who gets to hear his/her name boisterously emphasized by the group.

## Traffic Jam Variation

While we're talking about *The Traffic Jam* initiative problem, let me pass along a simple variation that I have been using with corporate groups, and one I think will work with any group has has been imbued with our society's competitive, win-or-else mentality.

Set up the problem so that you have two groups doing the same problem concurrently. Present the rules to the group as a whole; i.e., before you ask them to separate into two groups. Emphasize that you are not splitting the group into two competing teams, and encourage each group to **share** whatever they learn toward completion of the problem.

The results are predictable. Each group becomes very solicitous of what *they* have developed and become reluctant to share any progress they have achieved. The group that first comes up with the solution is usually glad to share their good fortune, however the still struggling group wants nothing to do with their largesse, preferring to "...come up with the answer ourselves." The various and sometimes unpredictable dynamics of this variation lend themselves to valuable, heated, and revealing discussions.

## Multiple Moonball — a variation with merit

Use this variation after the group has had some time with the basic hit-it-in-sequence game.

If your group numbers about 20, blow up 4-5 beach balls. All the balls are started (hit) at the same time, following the basic Moonball rules (*Bottomless Bag*, pg. 55). Each person who starts a particular ball must keep an accurate hit-count for that ball. When that ball finally makes contact with the ground, the counter mentally records the number. Play continues until ALL the balls have made contact with the ground. Each counter then reveals her/his respective total in order to gain a grand group score. Another attempt is then initiated (after a bit of discussion, recrimination, and quasi-constructive comments) to try and better that score.

With lots of bouncing balls available for hitting at the beginning of the game, there is not so much inclination for a shy participant to "hide." Hopefully, near the end of the game, most everyone will be interested in upping the final ball-strike total, and won't be reluctant to hit the ball(s) if it rebounds their way.

This useful variation was thunk-up by Dave Villandry of Cambridge, MA.

## Chapter Seven
# *Miscellaneous*

### Forehead-Slappers

Tom Krauska from St. Louis, MO, sent in these puzzlers. Even though I knew the questions were asked in a tricky way, and that the answers would be forehead-slappers, I still missed quite a few. (No, I didn't miss them all.) Here's a selection of the best.

1. What is at the end of infinity?

2. In Monopoly, if you started from Go and rolled a 2, a 12, and then a 2, where would you be?

3. Approximately how many grooves are there on each side of the average 12" 33 r.p.m. record?

4. John bought 7 apples and ate all but 3. How many were left?

5. An archaeologist found an object with the following description. What was the purpose of the object?

   Toti

   e

   hors

   esto

6. What do you sit on, sleep on, and brush your teeth with?

7. How many animals of each species did Moses take into the Ark?

8. Some months have 30 days. Some months have 31 days. How many months have 28 days?

9.  If you have a kerosene lamp and a candle and only one match, which do you light first?

10. How many 3 cent postcards in a dozen?

**Answers to 1-10:**

1.  The letter Y

2.  Jail...3 doubles

3.  One...continuous

4.  Three

5.  To tie horses to

6.  A chair, a bed, and a toothbrush.

7.  Moses didn't take any animals into the Ark

8.  They all have 28 days

9.  Always light the match first

10. 12...

## Demon Rings

Ever been hit by the flailing arms of a trusting faller? Ever seen the "hit" happen during the Trust Fall sequence? Unfortunately, the whacked nose or bruised cheek is bound to happen eventually, no matter how tightly the trouser material is gripped or fingers are interlocked. I've contemplated using long velcro bands around the chest area, and experimented with bungee cord wrapped around the wrists, but such voluntary bondage smacks of partial participation. So, during a June workshop that I was co-leading with Ken Demas, when Ken came up with the following simple solution to the occasional lateral karate-like chops that changed the Trust Fall to the Fend-Off Fall, I was delighted; so much so that I immediately named the rubber restraining bracelet — Demon Rings: Demon = Demas.

Take one of the rubber deck tennis rings that you use for the game *Italian Golf*, and slip it over the faller's hands, which are held in a palms-together, prayer-like position. Then, with the ring encircling the wrists, ask the faller to interlock his/her fingers. Even a person so unnerved by a backward fall from 5+ feet will not be able to extricate their hands during the short time span of the actual fall.

This ring/wrist arrangement will function well for comparatively large hands and wrists. For smaller hands, two rings may be necessary. Squeeze one ring slightly so that it fits inside the second ring. So arranged, the rings will be perpendicular to one another — not concentric. The hands are inserted into the obvious openings. Hello, Demon Rings. Goodbye, whacked faces.

## A Collection of "Things" That Have Changed...for those born before 1945

"We were born before television, before penicillin, before polio shots, frozen foods, Xerox, plastic, contact lenses, Frisbees, and **THE PILL**. We were before radar, credit cards, split atoms, laser beams, and ballpoint pens. Before pantyhose, dishwashers, clothes dryers, electric blankets, air conditioners, drip-dry clothes...and before man walked on the moon.

We got married first and **then** lived together. In our time, closets were for clothes, not for 'coming out of.' Bunnies were small rabbits, and rabbits were not Volkswagens.

We thought fast food was what you ate during Lent. We were before house husbands, gay rights, computer dating, dual careers, and computer marriages. We were before day-care centers, group therapy, and nursing homes. We never heard of FM radio, tape decks, electronic typewriters, artificial hearts, word processors, yogurt and guys wearing earrings. For us, time-sharing meant togetherness...not computers or condominiums. A chip meant a piece of wood. Hardware meant hardware, and software wasn't even a word.

Back then, 'Made in Japan' meant **junk** and the term 'making out' referred to how you did on your exam. Pizzas, McDonald's, and instant coffees were unheard of. We hit the scene where there were 5 and 10-cent stores where you bought things for five and ten cents. For one nickel, you could ride a street car, make a phone call, buy a Pepsi, or enough stamps to mail one letter **and** two postcards. You could buy a new Chevy coupe for $600...but who could afford one? A pity too, because gas was 11 cents a gallon!

In our day grass was mowed, **COKE** was a cold drink, and **POT** was something you cooked in. **ROCK MUSIC** was Grandma's lullaby and **AIDS** were helpers in the principal's office. We made do with what we had. And we were the last generation that was so dumb as to think you needed a husband to have a baby."

As we live from day to day, it's difficult to "step back" and digest how much change in the world is taking place — and the more we change, the faster we seem to change.

The first time I read the above quoted material, I could hardly believe that pizzas, instant coffee, television, etc., weren't always around. Think back to when you saw your first digital watch: it wasn't that long ago. I still don't know where the #'s come from.

The point is, things they are a-changin' and time's-a-wastin,' so if you had anything in mind to do, better get it done before it or you are out of style. Free-associate that one, and burn some daylight, good buddy, 'cause there's not a lot left.

## For Your Information Only

Why else would I include such esoteric information — unless you wanted to develop an advanced version of the game *Barnyard*. Nonetheless, this is need-to-know information for trivia buffs and worth a few "I-didn't-know-that's" from the rest of us.

| Animal | Male | Female | Young | Collective | Gestation | Longevity | (Record) |
|--------|------|--------|-------|------------|-----------|-----------|----------|
| Ass | Jack | Jenny | Foal | Herd | 340-385 | 18-20 | (63) |
| Bear | He-bear | She-bear | Cub | Sleuth | 180-240 | 18-20 | (34) |
| Cat | Tom | Queen | Kitten | Clutter/Clowder | 52-65 | 10-12 | (27) |
| Cattle | Bull | Cow | Calf | Drove/Herd | 280 | 9-12 | (25) |
| Chicken | Rooster | Hen | Chick | Brood/Clutch | 21 | 7-8 | (14) |
| Deer | Buck | Doe | Fawn | Herd | 140-250 | 10-15 | (26) |
| Dog | Dog | Bitch | Pup | Pack | 55-70 | 10-12 | (24) |
| Duck | Drake | Duck | Duckling | Brace/Herd | 21-35 | 10 | (15) |
| Elephant | Bull | Cow | Calf | Herd | 515-760 | 30-40 | (98) |
| Fox | Dog | Vixen | Cub/Kit | Skulk | 51-60 | 8-10 | (14) |
| Goat | Billy | Nanny | Kid | Tribe, Trip | 135-163 | 12 | (17) |
| Goose | Gander | Goose | Gosling | Flock/Gaggle | 30 | | |
| Horse | Stallion | Mare | Filly/Colt | Herd | 304-419 | 20-25 | (50+) |
| Lion | Lion | Lioness | Cub | Pride | 105-111 | 10 | (29) |
| Monkey | Male | Female | Boy/Girl | Band/Troop | 149-179 | 12-15 | (29) |
| Rabbit | Buck | Doe | Bunny | | 27-36 | 6-8 | (15) |
| Sheep | Ram | Ewe | Lamb | Flock/Drove | 121-180 | 12 | (16) |
| Swan | Cob | Pen | Cygnet | Bevy | 30 | | |
| Swine | Boar | Sow | Piglet | Litter | 101-130 | 10 | (15) |
| Tiger | Tiger | Tigress | Cub | | 105 | 19 | |
| Whale | Bull | Cow | Calf | Gam/Pod | 276-365 | 37 | |
| Wolf | Dog | Bitch | Pup | Pack | 63 | 10-12 | (16) |

## Maximum Pull-Ups

I have always been ritualistically one-minded about doing things that I thought were good for me, sometimes paradoxically injuring myself because of that penchant for compulsion. However, as the result of a full-year compulsive commitment, I am able to pass along some marginally positive results.

About 13 months ago, I was feeling a bit wimpy in the upper bod because of an exercise hiatus resulting from a bicycle accident. I said to myself; "*Self*, you need a major fitness goal to offset this insidious atrophy affliction." So I set a long term goal — to do 10,000 pull-ups over the next year; the calculator unsympathetically indicates a 27.4 per day requirement.

I just finished up this fiscal pull-up year on October 1, with a twelve month total of 16,150, which translates to 44.2 pull-ups per day. The fact that I achieved my personal goal isn't all that remarkable (just stubborn), but I wanted to pass along the physical and psychological results of this type of benign compulsion, because I doubt if I'll do it again.

I started off being able to max-out at maybe 15 regulation pull-ups. (We're talkin' pull-ups here, not chin-ups — i.e., palms away, not palms toward yourself.) I can do 26 pull-ups now, and maybe 28 on a real good day. So, incisive insight #1 is that my ability to do a greater number of pull-ups has increased markedly. Insight #2 is perhaps a bit more insightful. I found that being able to do 26 consecutive pull-ups has not helped me to do anything else better. (Actually, that's not true; paddling a canoe seems easier.) However, the discipline of doing a certain number of repetitive exercises and recording that number each day was undeniably satisfying. I felt better about myself every day after having completed my 24-hour requirement.

Now I'm into a new exercise program that isn't worth mentioning, but there is definitely more variety included. My suggestion to insure continuation of your own fitness scheme is to set a long term goal that is challenging (not impossible) and record your progress on a daily basis; it's infectious and if you pursue that goal with an exercise buddy, actually fun.

Since I had committed myself to a year-long goal, I thought someone else might like to join me; part of the shared-pain compulsion syndrome. So, I suggested that Project Adventure, Inc., offer each ropes course builder on our staff one penny for each pull-up they performed during the year (penny-a-pull-up), to a maximum of $100.00; i.e., 10,000 pull-ups. A few started, but Dave Klim was the only person to reach the 10,000 goal. I believe Dave started off being able to do 4 regulation pull-ups, and can now whip off 18. Additionally, and not significantly, Dave is also the only person I know of who has done a pull-up at over 30,000 ft.

I saw this brief notation in a magazine recently. "In 1918, at a gym in Philadelphia, Lillian Leitzel did 27 chin-ups with her right hand. She then did 19 chin-ups with her left hand. No one has ever equalled that feat." I give up Lillian — the record's all yours.

## The Sneaker Graveyard

Mud is a social leveller nonpareil, but it's also an entertaining tool for viscous immersion fun therapy.

Hamilton-Wenham Regional High School has the original and probably still the most outstanding Sneaker Graveyard around. The "graveyard" represents an impressive expanse of the best programmatic mud I've ever experienced. This particular organic (all natural) quivering bog extends beneath the length of a 40-foot long, kind-of-loose tension traverse cable. At certain times of year, it's hard to tell if there's any mud beneath the cable at all, but a couple errant steps in the wrong direction remind you that "knee deep" is not just a frog's greeting call.

The Sneaker Graveyard soubriquet was awarded early-on, because when a student slips off the cable in mid-passage, the force of the descent implants their feet (and sometimes other parts of the anatomy) deeply into the mud. Not wanting to linger and role play Rambo, the hapless wallower attempts to jerk their foot out of the mire and, more often than not, deposits a shoe approximately 18" below the surface. Reluctant to muck around looking for a shoe, the half-brown person quick-steps to more solid terra, losing another shoe in the less-than-firma.

Each winter, because of frost heaval, the implanted footwear inexorably makes its way to the surface of the mud and eventually reveals itself as a half-buried cockeyed headstone, proclaiming inaccurately the recent demise of a Mr. Adidas or Ms. Nike.

In the spring, I have counted upwards of 70 sneakers jutting out of the mud; enticing, yet warning the wobbling wire walker to take "just one more step."

## Riddle Games

To be honest, I've never liked these Who-Done-It? and How'd-They-Do-It? type of word problems, but my boys like them and so do other people, so here's a collection of them that I found recently. I wish I could remember where, because I like to give credit for this kind of stuff in *BOT's*. If you recognize this list as yours, thank you.

1. A woman gave a piece of food to the man she lived with. His eating of the food resulted in his death. Even though this event became world famous, she was never brought to trial. *The man and the woman were Adam and Eve.*

2. A man enters a bar in Chicago during the noon hour and asks the bartender for a drink of water. The bartender reaches under the counter, draws out a gun and points it at the man, who then says, "Thank you," turns around, and walks out. *The man had the hiccups; the bartender scared him.*

3. In a room is a table, some broken glass on the floor, and some water on the floor. Mary is dead. John is standing beside her. How did Mary die? *John is a cat; Mary is a goldfish. John pushed the bowl off the table.*

4. A man lives on the twenty-fifth floor in an apartment house. Each day he gets in the elevator, goes down to the lobby, and goes to work. Each evening he returns to the building, gets in the elevator, goes up to the fourteen floor, gets out of the elevator, and walks up the last ten flights. Why? *The man is a midget. He can't reach above the fourteenth floor button.*

5. A man who worked in a circus was found in his room — dead. Next to his bed was a gun and his cane, which had been sawed off at the bottom. What happened? *He was a blind midget clown. He thought he was growing taller because someone was cutting his cane shorter and shorter, so he committed suicide.*

6. Two men were bound and put into their car trunk following a robbery. In the morning, a passing person

112

hear noises coming from the trunk, and the two were found. One man had died and one was quite alive and unharmed. Why? *There was a spare tire in the trunk. One man had breathed the air.*

7. A woman, Mrs. Jones, was killed in a "skiing accident" in Switzerland. When Mr. Smith in Chicago read of her death, he called the police and said, "It was murder, and Mr. Jones is the culprit." How did he know? *Mr. Smith is a ticket agent and he sold Mr. Jones one round-trip ticket and one one-way ticket to Switzerland.*

8. There was a car accident. A man is killed in the crash and his son is critically injured. The boy is rushed to the hospital and is prepared for surgery. When the doctor comes in to operate and sees the boy, the doctor says, "I can't operate, that's my son!" *The doctor is the boy's mother.*

## Ecological Have You Evers...

Dr. Lee Gillis, professor extraordinaire at Georgia College, put together these have you ever...? type questions and added an ecological twist. Way to twist, Lee, nice idea. Kind of let's you know what we haven't been doing that we should have. Have you ever...

...recycled aluminum, glass, newspaper, car batteries, used motor oil?

...intentionally avoided disposable plates, cups, plastic forks, etc.?

...used a cloth towel rather than a paper towel, if you had the choice?

...used a glass instead of a Styrofoam cup?

...bought something used rather than something new?

...repaired something you could have thrown away?

...ridden in a fuel-efficient car? Or owned one?

...been to a farmer's market and bought something to eat?

...refused a plastic bag at the grocery store?

...put a water displacement device in your toilet?

...eaten a strictly vegetarian meal?

...gone a week without eating a meat product?

...used a rechargeable battery?

...weatherstripped a window or a door?

...been to a toxic waste site?

...started and maintained a compost area?

...stopped using an aerosol spray in favor of a pump?

...taken a hot shower with water heated by a solar device?

...chewed the same piece of gum two consecutive days? (gimme a break!)


**ACRONYM — A** **C**ontrived **R**eduction **O**f **N**omenclature **Y**ielding **M**nemonics

Considering the above, the following makes perfect sense. From the fertile mind of John Cohen; Wheaton College, Norton, MA.


**PROJECT — P**eople **R**eally **O**ften **J**ust **E**njoy **C**oming **T**ogether


**ADVENTURE — A**nd **D**oing **V**ery **E**xciting **N**utty **T**hings **U**sually **R**aises **E**nthusiasm


**Self-Concept — Gimme A Big 10**

Substantive evaluation questions — For those of you who are having so much fun you've forgotten why you're doing it. Doing what? I can't remember, but I like it.

I've had this evaluation scale sitting in the *BOT's* file for a long time, and I keep meaning to include it, so I did. Thanks to Leo Schettler of the Lorado Middle School in Aurora, CO, for sending this self-concept scale.

# Challenge Ropes Course

**Name** _____ **Date** _____

## Self-Concept Scale

Please circle the number that best tells how you see yourself in the following areas.
Number 1 means very low by your standards and Number 10 means almost perfect by your
standards.

### Trust In Others

Low        1      2      3      4      5      6      7      8      9      10

---

### Self-Confidence With People

Low        1      2      3      4      5      6      7      8      9      10

---

### Self-Confidence Challenging Physical Activities

Low        1      2      3      4      5      6      7      8      9      10

---

### Self-Confidence With School Work

Low        1      2      3      4      5      6      7      8      9      10

---

### Self-Confidence With Completing Difficult Tasks

Low        1      2      3      4      5      6      7      8      9      10

---

My Ability To Give Verbal Support To Others

Low       1    2    3    4    5    6    7    8    9    10

---

My Ability To Lead Others

Low       1    2    3    4    5    6    7    8    9    10

---

My Ability To Let Others Lead

Low       1    2    3    4    5    6    7    8    9    10

---

My Ability To Thank Others When They Do Things For Me

Low       1    2    3    4    5    6    7    8    9    10

---

My Ability To Solve Problems With A Group

Low       1    2    3    4    5    6    7    8    9    10

---

Peggy Meyer from Barrington, IL offers these following useful and insightful adventure-games teaching suggestions.

## Adventure Games Teaching Suggestions

1.  Establish relationships with the individual players right away.

2.  The key to including the slow-arrival is to continually extend an open and welcoming invitation to all new players.

3.  Establish yourself as a player as well as a leader right from the start.

4. Begin with games that provide easy access and have few, easily explained rules.

5. Let the players stretch their bodies and their feelings slowly at first.

6. Explain the game's structure and rules as clearly and simply as possible, and do it in a style that encourages participation, playfulness, fantasy and fun.

7. Combine description with demonstration.

8. Ask for questions. If a particular question suggests an interesting variation, you might use it as an opportunity to empower the players, allowing the group to take charge of the game.

9. Extend an invitation to play. Always give people choices.

10. If, as the leader, you are able to demonstrate the game with appropriately outrageous or foolish words and actions, you can serve as a model, encouraging all the players to cast aside their inhibitions and join you.

11. Before a physically active game, point out any qualities of the group's physical make-up that requires special safety procedures.

12. When presenting games, always look for opportunities to make the game fantasy or imagery come alive.

## Caffeine — The Generic Drug

Since the majority of our population ingests or imbibes caffeine in one way or another, here's a milligram comparison chart that allows you to know where the biggest "hit" is coming from. This data was gleaned from the University of California (Berkeley) Wellness Letter; 7/88. Interesting and nerve jangling.

### The daily dose

This chart will help you calculate your daily caffeine intake. But remember, caffeine content varies widely, depending on the product you use and how it's prepared.

| BEVERAGES | SERVING SIZE | CAFFEINE (mg) |
|---|---|---|
| Coffee, drip | 5 oz | 110-150 |
| Coffee, perk | 5 oz | 60-125 |
| Coffee, instant | 5 oz | 40-105 |
| Coffee, decaffeinated | 5 oz | 2-5 |
| Tea, 5-minute steep | 5 oz | 40-100 |
| Tea, 3-minute steep | 5 oz | 20-50 |
| Hot cocoa | 5 oz | 2-10 |
| Coca-Cola | 12 oz | 45 |

| FOODS | SERVING SIZE | CAFFEINE (mg) |
|---|---|---|
| Milk chocolate | 1 oz | 1-15 |
| Bittersweet chocolate | 1 oz | 5-35 |
| Chocolate cake | 1 slice | 20-30 |

| OVER-THE-COUNTER DRUGS | DOSE | CAFFEINE (mg) |
|---|---|---|
| Anacin, Empirin, or Midol | 2 | 64 |
| Excedrin | 2 | 130 |
| NoDoz | 2 | 200 |
| Aqua-Ban (diuretic) | 2 | 200 |
| Dexatrim (weight control aid) | 1 | 200 |

117

## Debunking Bananas

I feel obliged to report this shocking news about bananas because I have operated for years under the assumption that these plumpish golden rods of nutrition held all the potassium that a struggling bicyclist would ever need. And now I find (via a well know news publication) that there are beau coup edibles that have far more of this electrolyte than bananas provide. Check it out.

| | |
|---|---|
| **bananas** | 451 mg. |
| potato (baked) | 844 mg |
| cantaloupe (half) | 825 mg. |
| avocado (half) | 602 mg. |
| watermelon | 559 mg. (I always thought watermelon was for the pits.) |
| tomato juice (8 oz.) | 536 mg. |
| orange juice (8 oz.) | 473 mg. |
| etc., etc., etc. | |

The validity of banana use continues to be validated on Sesame Street however, by those well known erudite gourmands, Bert and Ernie.

Bert queries Ernie "Why do you have that banana sticking out of your ear?" Ernie replies ingenuously, "Bananas are known to repel alligators." Bert rejoinders derisively, "That's ridiculous, there's no alligators around here." Ernie looks at Bert knowingly and answers, "See?."

## Fitness

Ready to get rid of some winter fat and improve your c/v efficiency? Here's a handy formula that lets you know how hard to prime the pump or how hard you don't have to exercise to maintain a lifelong fitness level.

To figure out your maximum heart range while exercising, take 220 beats per minute and subtract your age in years and then multiply that answer by .6 to get the lower of the two numbers that make up the range. Then take 220 again and subtract your age, but this time multiply by .8 to get the higher number.

For example, at 53 years old, my range (rounded off) is 100-133. So during a 3-4 times per week, twenty minute exercise stint (rowing, stationary bike, etc.), all I have to do is keep my heartbeat within the above b.p.m. (beats per minute) range in order to maintain a functional fitness level.

## Abstract Symbols

Show me symbols like the ones below and ask me what I see, and I'll invariably see black abstracts. But then say, look beyond the black, and concentrate on the white, and what do you see; the *raison* for looking, of course. Once I have conceptualized the white symbols, it's hard for me to return to the black. Have a visual go at this yourself.

Are you having trouble "seeing?" Look at the white spaces between the black symbols. The white spaces spell a three letter word. See it? Don't let it **bug** you. That's a hint, ...I say that's a hint, son.

## Another Group Split Ploy

Ever notice that after you eat asparagus your urine smells funny? The distinctive odor that results from your body having processed the chemicals in asparagus is a genetic trait; i.e., some people's urine produces this strong indescribable odor and some don't. If you do (I do), there is no doubt in your mind (via the olfactory nerve) that you are one of these intrinsically talented folks. If you don't, schmooze around asking what your urine is supposed to smell like; gives you something meaningful to talk about at a gathering. Nonetheless, asking a group to split on a smell/no smell basis adds to your repertoire of genetic oddities for the large group game, *Categories*, and, of course, adds to your frequently manifested off-the-wall image.

The group split via urine aroma offered above borders on the offensive — know your group before asking them to commit to this type of revelation. No matter now interesting your topic of comparison is, if people are offended by your topic, their trust in you as a leader will diminish.

## What Are You Trying To Accomplish?

The above question can be couched in a number of ways, and the askers vary from concerned parents to corporate executives. When people ask, this is what I tell them.

"When I play with people in a games, curriculum, skills, technical, corporate, or whatever workshop, I ask them to:

- *Cooperate* — Try to make things work,

- *Communicate* — Talk about what's going on without fear of being put down,

- *Trust* — Physically and emotionally, without the worry of harm or embarrassment,

- Accept *fun* and *challenge* as a vehicle for personal growth,

- and *Commit* to all the above,"

toward building a hands-on vehicle for personal and group happiness. If you and others are happy with the situation and one another, good things happen. So make them happen!

## Chapter Eight
# *Quarterly Quotes*

I am becoming a compulsive quote quoter. When I hear or read something that appeals to me I write it down, record it on a micro recorder, rip or cut it out of an airline magazine or, in extremis, attempt to memorize it until I can do one of the above. After I collect a bunch, I read through them a few times and cull out the ones that were obviously of passing interest only. The remainder are what you see here.

That section of **Bag of Tricks** called *Quarterly Quotes* is something I include for myself. I hope you enjoy these one-liners and aphorisms as much as I do, and hopefully you will find an occasional use for just the right zinger, rationalization, or inspiration in your own pedagogic pursuits.

"If you can bring a little bit of fun into people's lives, then it's worth it."

*Gene Hackman*

"I want to do something that is not necessarily wise and prudent, I want to have some fun."

*George Allen*

"The way to succeed is to double your failure rate."

*IBM founder Tom Watson*

"If you learn that failing even a little bit penalizes you (being wrong only 15% of the time gets you only a B grade), you learn not to make mistakes, and, more significantly, you learn to not put yourself into positions where you might fail."

*Roger von Oech*

"Children enter school as question marks and leave as periods."

*Neil Postman*

"It's better to light some candles and wear all black and whirl around and chant incomprehensible lyrics and then whirl around some more than to curse the darkness."

*MTV babble*

"If our delivery vans careen around the corner and smack into your auto at wildly excessive speeds, we guarantee we'll deliver you to a hospital within thirty minutes."

*Domino's Pizza parody via National Lampoon magazine*

"Total 1988 ticket receipts for U.S. movie theaters: $4.46 billion."

*Conde Nast Traveler magazine*

"A mistake is just another way of doing things."

*Anonymous*

"My isolation is the darkroom where I develop my negatives"

*Anonymous*

"I hang onto my prejudices, they are the testicles of my mind."

*Eric Hoffer*

"I have a new philosophy; I'm only going to dread one day at a time."

*Charles M Schultz*

"Adulthood is a depressing destination. As you grow up, you become adulterated."

*C.W. Metcalf*

Six-Year-Old #1: "Did you see the condom on the patio?"
Six-Year-Old #2: "What's a patio?"

*Anonymous*

"It takes a very rainy day to drown a duck."

*Charlie Chan*

"You can't have everything – where would you put it?"

*Anonymous*

"I used to think I was tenacious and dedicated until I discovered the word stubborn."

*Anne Schaef*

"For the longest time I never believed I was an alcoholic. I was so into denial I convinced myself that I was a stunt man for Cutty Sark."

*John Paul Cookley*

"If it is worth doing, it is worth doing wrong until you get it right."

*Dean C.*

"I had a lot of husbands, but none of them were mine."

*Diane C.*

"They think children are cement for a crumbling marriage. They're not, they're hand grenades."

*Person in counseling*

"A dead atheist is someone who's all dressed up with no place to go."

*James Daffecy*

"An atheist is a person who has no invisible means of support."

*Fulton J. Sheen*

"I wear a peacock suit, but underneath there's a turkey."
"I thought I was in the driver's seat, but I wasn't even in the car."
"I'm still crazy as hell, but if I don't drink or use drugs, nobody will notice."

*Recovering mental health patients*

"Life is a sexually transmitted disease."

*Guy Bellamy*

"The difference between genius and stupidity is that genius has its limits."

*Anonymous*

"While we may not be unavoidably cooperative or unavoidably competitive, we are, at worst, not unavoidably anything at all."

*Alfie Kohn*


"In so far as man is concerned, if competition, in its combative aggressive sense, ever had any adaptive value among men, it is quite clear that it has no adaptive value whatever in the modern world... Perhaps never before in the history of mankind has there been so high a premium upon the adaptive value of cooperative behavior."

*Ashley Montagu*


"The war between the sexes is the only one in which both sides regularly sleep with the enemy."

*Quentin Crisp*


"Thousands have lived without love, not one without water."

*W.H. Auden*


"Women aren't embarrassed when they buy men's pajamas, but a man buying a nightgown acts as though he were dealing with a dope peddler."

*Jimmy Cannon*


"...competing simply means that one is working toward a goal in such a way as to prevent others from reaching *their* goals."

*Alfie Kohn*


"We destroy the love of learning in children, which is so strong when they are small, by encouraging and compelling them to work for petty and contemptible rewards - gold stars, or papers marked 100 and tacked to the wall, or A's on report cards, or honor rolls, or dean's lists — in short, for the ignoble satisfaction of feeling that they are better than someone else."

*John Holt*


"...each individual in a crowd is able to see better by standing on tip toe, particularly when others are doing so. But everyone would do better if no one stood on tip toe."

*Economist Fred Hirsch*

"In the state of nature, most objects come in a form that can be shared by a large number of people... Uniqueness seems to be invented by humans, who invent activities deliberately designed to allow entry into the goal region to one individual only."

*Emmy Pepitone*


"If it weren't for pickpockets, I'd have no sex life at all."

*Rodney Dangerfield*


Biological definition of a kiss — Two people sucking on the end of a tube 33 feet long and one third filled with fecal matter.

*Dr. Crystal Schlatz*


"If love is the answer, could you rephrase the question?

*Lily Tomlin*


"Man is proud that he has the biggest brain of all the primates, but attempts to conceal that he also has the biggest penis."

*Desmond Morris*


Pertaining to the idea of pursuing competition at an early age to condition the child to occasional losses and failure...
"The idea that we are best prepared for unpleasant experiences by being exposed to unpleasant experiences at a tender age is about as sensible as the proposition that the best way to help someone survive exposure to carcinogenic substances is to expose him to as many carcinogens as possible early in life."

*Alfie Kohn*


"Work is difficult; that's why it's called work."

*David Brown*


"Women, can't live with them, can't shoot them."

*Stephen Wright*


"A truly wise man never plays leapfrog with a unicorn."

*"Banacek"*

"If you forget how to tie a bowline, tie lots of whatever knot you remember."

                                        *KER*

"It doesn't matter if you win or lose, it's how well you accept my winning."

                                        *KER*

"Find out what you don't do well, then don't do it."

                                        *"Alf"*

"A hard man is good to find."

                                        *Mae West*

"Sex is good, but not as good as fresh sweet corn."

                                        *Garrison Keillor*

"When I was a kid, my parents moved a lot, but I always found them."

                                        *Rodney Dangerfield*

"With regard to ham and eggs: The chicken is involved, the pig is committed."

                                        *Anonymous*

"Don't think! Thinking is the enemy of creativity."

                                        *Ray Bradbury*

"In Mexico we have a word for sushi:  bait."

                                        *Jose Simon*

"Smoking is one of the leading causes of statistics."

                                        *Fletcher Knebel*

"A vegetarian is a person who won't eat anything that can have children."

                                        *David Brenner*

"Life is just a bag of tricks."

                                        *"Felix the Cat"*

"Showing up is 90% of success."

*Anonymous*

"I never believed in Santa Claus, because I knew no white dude would come into my neighborhood after dark."

*Dick Gregory*

"When I was in the third grade, there was a kid running for office. His slogan was: 'Vote for me and I'll show you my wee-wee.' He won by a landslide."

*Dorothy Zbornack*

"I got nothin' against mankind.  It's people I can't stand."

*Archie Bunker*

"Never argue with people who buy ink by the gallon."

*Tommy Lasorda*

"If olive oil comes from olives, then where does baby oil come from?"

*Jane Wagner*

"Roses are red, violets are blue, I'm schizophrenic and so am I.

*Frank Crow*

"If you shoot a mime, should you use a silencer?"

*Stephen Wright*

"The lion and the calf shall lie down together, but the calf won't get much  sleep."

*Woody  Allen*

"Some of us are becoming the men we wanted to marry."

*Gloria Steinem*

"You gotta know the rules before you can break 'em.  Otherwise, it's just no  fun."

*Miami Vice actor*

"Experience is not what happens to you, it's what you **do** with what happens to you."

Ken Blanchard

"If we don't change our direction we are likely to end up where we're headed."

Ancient Chinese proverb

"One of the things we pride ourselves on is doing things consistently different."

John Lazarus

"Somewhere on this globe every ten seconds, there is a woman giving birth to a child. She must be found and stopped.

Sam Levinson

"...when I commit to providing an adventure activity for the students, I imagine I've stepped off the zip wire platform — the ride has begun and there is no way to stop it. This concept has helped me to keep going when seemingly insurmountable problems arise and I must remind myself to enjoy the ride."

Jo Ann Freer

"The most difficult tongue twister — "The sixth six sheik's sixth sheep's sick."

Guiness Book of World Records

"A one pound ball of steel dropped into the water above the deepest part of the ocean (Marianas Trench – 6.79 miles) would take almost 64 minutes to reach the ocean floor."

Scientific American

"If you are a rock climber, your friends probably regard you with suspicion. Any form of striving that once made people heros — any quest that carries acceptance of risk — now makes them crazies.

To sustain comfort, we have to be safe — safe from confrontation with other people, objects or elements. In a comfortable world, the hard edges have been padded, rounded or smoothed — it's the home of the foam rubber lawn mower. But where there is no risk, there is no achievement."

Reader's Digest

128

"Son," the old man said, "as soon as you go around and about in this world, some day you will come upon a man who will lay down in front of you a new deck of cards with the seal unbroken and offer to bet he can make the jack of spades jump out of the deck and squirt cider in your ear." "Son," the old man continued, "do not bet him, because as soon as you do, you are going to get an earful of cider."

*Damon Runyon "Black bugs blood"*
*Alice Campbell*


"I believe I've found the missing link between animal and civilized man. It is us."

*Konrad Lorenz*


"Societies that do not eat people are fascinated by those that do."

*Ronald Wright*


"Faith may be defined briefly as an illogical belief in the occurrence of the improbable."

*H.L. Mencken*


"On one side, people of normal human appetites, on the other, those who crave only the roar and crackle of their own neurons, whipped into a frenzy of synthetic euphoria."

*Newsweek article on CRACK abuse: 11/88*


"It's not that I'm afraid to die, I just don't want to be there when it happens."

*Woody Allen*


"People who keep attack dogs are cowards who haven't got the guts to bite people themselves."

*August Strindberg*


"There's one store called Bon Jour Croissant. It makes me want to go to Paris and open a store called Hello Toast."

*Fran Lebowitz*

"Fork – n. An instrument used chiefly for the purpose of putting dead animals into the mouth."

*Ambrose Bierce*

"When people are free to do as they please, they usually imitate one another."

*Eric Hoffer*

"If you can't say anything good about someone, sit right here by me."

*Alice Roosevelt Longworth*

"When I told the people of Northern Ireland that I was an atheist, a woman in the audience stood up and said, 'Yes, but is it the God of the Catholics or the God of the Protestants in whom you don't believe?'"

*Quintin Crisp*

"History is a set of lies agreed upon."

*Napoleon Bonaparte*

"History would be a wonderful thing — if it were only true."

*Leo Tolstoy*

"Immorality:  the morality of those who are having a better time."

*H.L. Mencken*

"Laziness is nothing more than the habit of resting before you get tired."

*Jules Renard*

"It is always the best policy to tell the truth, unless, of course, you are an exceptionally good liar."

*Jerome K. Jerome*

"I figure you have the same chance of winning the lottery whether you play or not."

*Fran Lebowitz*

In response to the question, Why?, posed by Groucho Marx of a woman who had given birth to 22 children, she explained sheepishly, "I love my husband." Groucho's reply. "I love my cigar too, but I take it out once in a while."

"Principles have no real force except when one is well fed."

*Mark Twain*

"The trouble with the rat race is that even if you win, you're still a rat."

*Lily Tomlin*

"I took a speed reading course and read *War and Peace*. It involves Russia."

*Woody Allen*

"Suburbia is where the developer bulldozes out the trees, then names the streets after them."

*Anonymous*

"It is not enough to succeed; others must fail."

*Gore Vidal*

"So little time, so little to do."

*Oscar Levant*

"By working faithfully eight hours a day, you may eventually get to be a boss and work twelve hours a day."

*Robert Frost*

"If the world were a logical place, men would ride side-saddle."

*Rita Mae Brown*

"There are 100,000,000,000,000,000,000,000 estimated stars in the universe, and 5776 stars visible to the naked eye."

*The Book of Comparisons*

"Positive anything is better than negative nothing."

*Hubbard*

"He who will not answer to the rudder must answer to the rocks."

*Herve*

"Many would be cowards if they had nerve enough."

*Anonymous*

"He was a bold man who first ate an oyster."

*Swift*

"Never give up on someone until they fail at something they like."

*Lewis Lawes*

"Thrusting my nose firmly between his teeth, I threw him heavily to the ground on top of me."

*Mark Twain*

"Immigration is the sincerest form of flattery."

*Anonymous*

"Never forget what a person says to you when they are angry."

*H.W. Butler*

"God will not look you over for medals, degrees or diplomas but for scars."

*Elbert Hubbard*

"She has a nice sense of rumor."

*John Cutler*

"The cat is in the parlor, the dog is in the lake;
The cow is in the hammock — what difference does it make?"]

*Anonymous*

Being asked whether it was better to marry or not, Socrates replied, "Whichever you do you will repent it."

*Diogenes Laertius*

"My memory is the thing I forget with."

*A child's definition*

"Going sailing is like being in jail with the chance of drowning."

*Paraphrase from a Samuel Johnson quote*

"Women (Men) should be obscene and not heard."

*Groucho Marx*

"Television is now so desperately hungry for material that they're scraping the top of the barrel."

*Gore Vidal*

"Game over, Man! Game Over!

*Pvt. Hudson — The movie Aliens*

"If I'm going to be challenged, I'd rather it be while I'm comfortable."

*KER*

"Children should neither be seen or heard — ever again."

*W.C. Fields*

"The secret of dealing successfully with a child is not to be its parent."

*Mell Lazarus*

"Children make the most desirable opponents in Scrabble as they are both easy to beat and fun to cheat."

*Fran Lebowitz*

"Also, just beyond the horizon is the threat of the cinema and television, which require only a little popularizing before they too will invade the forecastle; when they do the sailor's hands will once again be idle."

*Ashley's Book of Knots — Copyright 1944*

"The other day I told my players, 'Isn't it great to be a winner? I want you to put this on your resume.'"

*George Allen*

"Challenge by Contract," or "Full Value Choice"?

*KER*

# BOTTOMLESS BAGGIE
## INDEX